T0301351

Sick of Inequality?

An Introduction to the Relationship between Inequality and Health

Andreas Bergh

Lund University and Research Institute of Industrial Economics, Sweden

Therese Nilsson

Lund University and Research Institute of Industrial Economics, Sweden

Daniel Waldenström

Research Institute of Industrial Economics, Sweden and Paris School of Economics, France

Cheltenham, UK • Northampton, MA, USA

© Andreas Bergh, Therese Nilsson and Daniel Waldenström 2016

This book is a revised and expanded version of the Swedish book *Blir vi sjuka av inkomstskillnader?* (Studentlitteratur, 2012).

Published by
Edward Elgar Publishing Limited
The Lypiatts
15 Lansdown Road
Cheltenham
Glos GL50 2JA
UK

Edward Elgar Publishing, Inc.
William Pratt House
9 Dewey Court
Northampton
Massachusetts 01060
USA

A catalogue record for this book
is available from the British Library

Library of Congress Control Number: 2016938582

This book is available electronically in **Elgar**online
Economics subject collection
DOI 10.4337/9781785364211

ISBN 978 1 78536 420 4 (cased)
ISBN 978 1 78536 421 1 (eBook)

Typeset by Servis Filmsetting Ltd, Stockport, Cheshire
Printed and bound by CPI Group (UK) Ltd, Croydon, CR0 4YY

Contents

Acknowledgement

Financial support from the Swedish Research Council and the Torsten Söderberg's Foundation (Bergh and Nilsson) is gratefully acknowledged. The authors would also like to thank Karin Lindell, Emma de Graaf and Hanna Thunström for excellent research assistance.

1. Introduction

Imagine a household so poor that 90 per cent of all households in the same country have higher disposable incomes. By how much would the income of this particular household have to increase to place it among the top 10 per cent of households? The answer depends on the country in which the household resides. In Sweden, its disposable income would have to triple to move from the lowest 10 per cent to the highest 10 per cent. This may sound like a large change, but by international standards, Sweden is a nation with very little income inequality. The household's income would have to be multiplied by four in Germany and by six in the USA. In Colombia, the household's income would have to be increased by a factor of 11 to move from the bottom tenth percentile to the top tenth. In other words, the extent of income inequality varies drastically across countries.

There are also large differences in life expectancy across countries. Life expectancy at birth is 81 years in Sweden, 79 in Germany, 78 in the USA and only 73 in Colombia. If the data for these countries are plotted in a graph with income inequality on the horizontal axis and life expectancy on the vertical, a pattern arises: people in societies with greater income inequality tend to live shorter lives (see Figure 1.1).

The correlation in Figure 1.1 certainly provides food for thought. Do people in societies with higher levels of income inequality always have shorter life expectancies? Do people who earn exactly the same incomes but live in different countries have different health statuses? Do these patterns mean that income inequality is unhealthy? To what degree does being significantly poorer than the other three countries reduce life expectancy in Colombia? Do these patterns hold if we measure health and income inequalities differently? These topics will all be addressed in this book.

A few decades ago, a group of scholars set out to investigate the idea that social comparisons are determinants of individual health in wealthy countries. This idea formed the basis for a series of studies

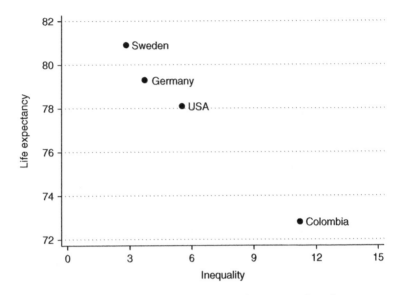

Note: The measure of income inequality is the P90/P10 measure from the Luxembourg Income Study. The measure of life expectancy is from the World Development Indicators (WDI). In Chapter 2, we detail various measures of population and individual health, while we review and discuss additional measures of income inequality in Chapter 3.

Figure 1.1   Life expectancy and income inequality in four countries in 2005

on the health of officials at Whitehall, which houses various British government agencies (Marmot et al., 1984, 1991). The researchers initially believed that the tough pace of work and the demanding responsibilities of the senior employees would lead to high stress and decreased health. However, the opposite results were obtained: the health of those at the bottom of the hierarchy suffered the most. These results could not be explained by behavioural patterns, such as smoking or other deleterious habits; rather, one's relative position within the work-related hierarchy was a key factor determining health.

These studies spurred others to inquire further about socioeconomic gradients in health. Economic historian and epidemiologist Richard Wilkinson explored a related but distinct hypothesis that income inequality in a society is harmful to *everyone's* health regardless of whether they are located at the top or at the bottom of the income distribution. Together with Kate Pickett, Wilkinson received worldwide attention for the book *The Spirit Level* (Wilkinson and Pickett, 2009). They argue that in rich countries, the income distribution plays a larger role in health outcomes than does the actual level of income and that those differences in income cause bad health.[1]

Scientific research on the relationship between income distribution and various measures of health has grown impressively large: hundreds of studies and reports address this question, spanning academic fields, in particular, medicine (social medicine, epidemiology), sociology and economics.[2] Despite these efforts, and perhaps contrary to the impression one forms from the public debate, research in this area is progressing, although consensus has not been reached on several central issues: How persuasive is the evidence of an inequality effect? If this effect exists, how large is it? Is the relationship causal, or are there other factors that explain why high inequality and adverse health outcomes tend be associated? Does the relationship between inequality and health exist in every type of society, and what kinds of health issues are affected? Which mechanisms cause an unequal income distribution to lead to poor health? How is health affected in a society if everyone grows richer as income inequality increases?

The purpose of this book is to discuss the state of the research addressing the relationship between inequality and health. In particular, we wish to explain the difficulties involved in identifying the effect of inequality on health and to present the ways in which one can measure this effect robustly. We provide a comprehensive review of the latest cross-disciplinary academic literature, identifying common patterns that offer at least partial answers to the above questions and provide directions for fruitful future research.

This book is structured as follows. After this introduction, eight chapters are followed by a lengthy appendix that provides an

---

[1] *The Spirit Level* was not the first book published by Wilkinson on the relationship between inequality and health. The same theme is explored in *Mind the Gap: Hierarchies, Health and Human Evolution* (2000) and in *Unhealthy Societies: The Affliction of Inequality* (1996). Wilkinson's hypothesis in all of these works is that inequality in society is detrimental to everyone – not just the poor.

[2] In a recent article, Pickett and Wilkinson (2015) note that as many as 300 peer-reviewed studies (including both population studies using aggregate data and studies using individual-level data) examine the income inequality hypothesis (IIH).

extensive list of articles covered in the literature review. The first two chapters address measurement. Chapter 2, *Measuring health*, and Chapter 3, *Measuring inequality*, discuss the most commonly used measures of health and income inequality used by scholars today. We discuss the concepts that these measures are meant to capture and evaluate how well they do so.

In the next three chapters, we carefully analyse how researchers can demonstrate the connection between inequality and health. Chapter 4 – *How can economic inequality influence health?* – identifies some of the central theoretical mechanisms that could explain a negative correlation between inequality and health. The nature of each mechanism differs: some focus on psychosocial processes, some stress the importance of money, while others focus on politics, crime or other societal processes. Chapter 5, *Correlation or causality? Interpreting scatter plots and regressions*, provides a review of the empirical methods used by most scholars addressing this topic. Concepts such as correlation and causality are examined, as are the requirements for empirically deducing statistically significant causal relationships between inequality and health. To illustrate these methods, the authors present a statistical analysis intended to help readers who are not familiar with statistics to understand the basics of the research being discussed. Chapter 6 – *The ecological fallacy: what conclusions can be drawn from group averages?* – argues that basing one's analysis on aggregate data, which are often national averages, is insufficient; it is also crucial to access data based on individuals. Most previous studies have used only aggregate data, which significantly reduces their usefulness. This limitation is discussed further below.

Chapter 7 – *Income inequality and health: what does the literature tell us?* – presents an extensive summary of the state of the current research. We establish that the body of literature on inequality and health is sizeable. The number of relevant articles is significantly smaller, however, if you limit yourself to studies that analyse this relationship using individual-level data. The summary separates the studies into categories based on their measure of health (objective or subjective health), time perspective (immediate or delayed effects), geographic area (within countries or cross-national) and distributional differences (everyone in society is affected or the poor are primarily affected). The chapter closes with a discussion of the main conclusions one can draw from evaluating the current research. Chapter 8 – *Searching for the inequality effect: what tools are appropriate?* – discusses the reasons behind the often-conflicting results reported in the literature and suggests that the field would benefit from a closer correspondence between the mechanisms examined and the measure of inequality used to evaluate the results. In Chapter 9, *Conclusion*, the book is summarized, and the authors outline some crucial points on the overall question of whether differences in income make us sick.

A particular challenge in writing a book like this is that the alleged inequality effect has been analysed by scholars working in a variety of scientific disciplines – in both medical and social sciences. For example, focusing on the income distribution may be viewed as restrictive. Some cross-national social scientists argue that income inequality is merely an indicator that captures important aspects of the ecological setting of a society; this ecology rather than the income inequality itself either fosters or harms individual health. As we stress in this book, the relevant mechanisms may be several and complex, working through different channels and dimensions of inequality. In fact, this issue is so important that we devote an entire chapter to discussing which mechanisms may mediate a potential relationship between inequality and health.

Cross-disciplinary differences may also become visible in the use of statistical methods for assessing the inequality effect. Most scholars, regardless of discipline, tend to interpret their results in causal terms; however, we argue that such claims require that researchers use statistical techniques that identify causal effects.

Overall, we strongly believe that different research traditions can offer valuable insights and that we may learn a great deal from each other's methods and results. The encompassing approach of this book and the research summary examines the results of studies from all relevant fields, and we hope that it will make a constructive contribution to our understanding of one of the most important issues in our societies.

2.   Measuring health

To examine the relationship between income inequality and health, it is necessary to obtain balanced and representative measures of these variables. Identifying such measures may seem difficult, but in fact, the problem is quite the opposite, as numerous measures that mirror both inequality and health are available. The difficulty, therefore, is choosing which of these measures is most suitable for an investigation.

In this chapter and the next, we present the most commonly used measures of health and inequality utilized by scholars and discuss their usefulness for capturing the relevant aspects of the concepts they are supposed to capture. We begin with measures of health, which are often divided into *objective measures* and *subjective measures*. At times, the review may seem overly focused on details and impenetrable, but there is a purpose to this arrangement, as the selection of measures can have a major impact on the results of a scientific study. Realizing the importance of using appropriate and accurate measures is crucial to interpreting and assessing the existing research. As we show below, the observed relationship between economic inequality and individual health may depend on which health measures are used.

2.1   OBJECTIVE HEALTH MEASURES

Of all possible health measures, a few are difficult to argue against. For instance, it is not usually difficult to establish whether a person is dead or alive. Additionally, there is generally no real debate as to which of these conditions – dead or alive – is preferable. So-called *objective measures of health*, such as mortality, thus have the advantage of being precise and capturing many crucial aspects of health even if they do not capture everything that we think of as part of good health. These measures are objective in the sense that anyone can use them in a real-life setting and reach the same conclusions about their results. Commonly used objective measures of general health include life expectancy, infant mortality and risk of dying from a particular disease. Objective measures of other aspects of individual health, such as hypertension, chronic conditions, blood pressure and body mass index (BMI), also exist. For example, BMI is a measure of the relationship between the weight and height of an individual that tells us whether the person is overweight. Furthermore, height-for-age measures the correlation between height and age and is used to determine whether a child is growing at a normal pace during its first years of life. Some studies also use the consumption of prescribed pharmaceuticals as an objective health measure (see, for example, Schaller and Stevens, 2015; Mayer and Osterle, 2015).

Objective measures are not without their problems. For example, no consensus exists about which BMI values define an individual as over- or underweight. Likewise, whether BMI is even a valid measure of health is debated (see, for example, the discussion in Burkhauser and Cawley, 2008). According to recent medical literature, BMI may even be a misleading indicator of health, as it does not differentiate between fat and muscle – generating concern that BMI is a deficient measure of body fat – or provide any information about where fat is located on the body.

A further challenge to finding good proxies for health is that most studies use information about chronic conditions, height and weight that are reported by the patient.[1] Thus, there is a risk that the results are misleading to the extent that people do not answer correctly, which can occur for various reasons, especially if this misreporting misstates the prevalence of a chronic disease, the BMI value or the prevalence of obesity. A recent body of literature analyses the reliability of self-reported objective health measures, and there are several indications that objective measures suffer from error and bias (see, for example, Baker et al., 2004; Ljungvall et al., 2015).[2] Two kinds of measurement error can exist in objective health measures: people may report having a problem that they do not have (for example, they are not telling the truth, they have self-diagnosed their disease or they misunderstand their ailment) or people with a particular condition may not reveal it in a survey.

---

[1] This challenge always applies to subjective health measures, but it also applies to several objective health measures.
[2] As shown by Ljungvall et al. (2015), misreporting of height and weight also tends to vary systematically across socioeconomic groups and, in particular, among women.

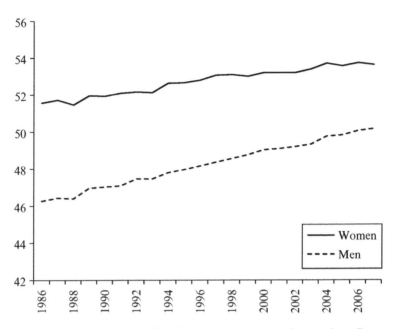

Source: Statistics Sweden (Statistics Sweden is a governmental agency that collects
data and produces statistics on different aspects of Swedish society).

*Figure 2.1   Expected remaining years of life for men and women at
              age 30*

We will now present and discuss examples of commonly used objective measures of population health in order to illustrate that these
measures can tell different stories about the inequality relationship
depending on how they are presented and across which groups
aggregation is chosen.

Figure 2.1 shows one of the most commonly used objective health
measures: statistically remaining life expectancy at age 30 (here, the
measure is shown for Swedish men and women over the 1986–2008
period).[3] A number of interesting facts can be seen in the graph. For
instance, although females tend to live longer than males, everyone's
life expectancy seems to increase over time, and the difference in
life expectancy between men and women seems to shrink over time.

---

[3]   As life expectancy at birth is heavily influenced by infant mortality, life expectancy
is often reported at a certain age (in our case, 30 years).

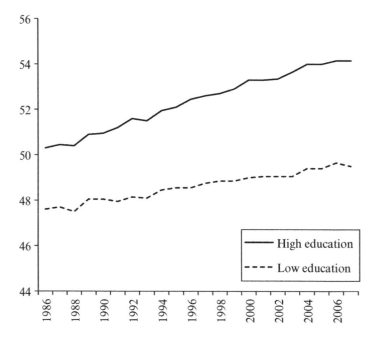

Source: Statistics Sweden.

Figure 2.2 Expected remaining years of life at age 30 by level of education

In general, life expectancy is increasing, and gender inequality in general health has decreased – which are both positive developments from most perspectives.

If we instead study trends in life expectancy between individuals without a high-school diploma (low education) with those who have post-secondary educations (higher education), the picture changes considerably. This relationship is shown in Figure 2.2. Although life expectancy has increased for both educational groups, the improvement has been more rapid among those with higher levels of education. Consequently, health inequality between these two groups has increased over time.[4]

In Figure 2.3 we divide the population further – according to

---

[4]   Vågerö (2011) shows that this increase in health inequality due to differences in levels of education has been occurring since at least the beginning of the 1970s.

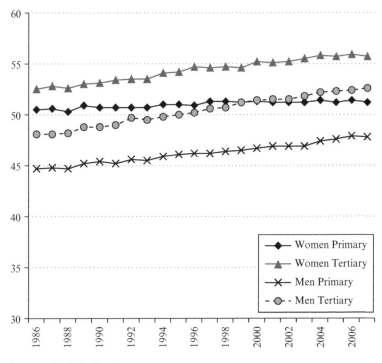

Source: Statistics Sweden.

*Figure 2.3   Expected remaining years of life at age 30 for men and
             women by level of education*

both gender and level of education. As shown previously, the difference in life expectancy between men and women decreases over
time, while the difference by education increases. In this setting,
however, it becomes clear that life expectancy for women with low
levels of education has hardly improved at all over the past decades.
Based on this pattern, we can conclude that the increase in life
expectancy among women with high levels of education drives the
increase in life expectancy for women as a whole. In addition to a
between-gender difference, there is a *within*-gender difference by
level of education. It should be noted, however, that the relative size
and composition of the groups varies over time, which is not shown
in the graphs. Women without high-school education, as a group,

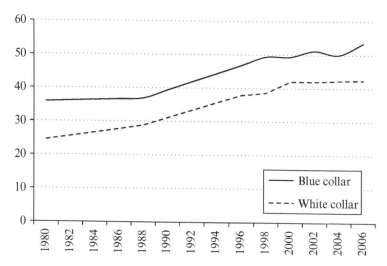

Note: Data were gathered for two years. The year shown in the diagram is the first of these years, except for 2004 and 2006, as there was a different data-gathering period.

Source: Statistics Sweden, Studies on Standard of Living [Undersökningarna av levnadsförhållanden (ULF)].

Figure 2.4   *Proportion of overweight people among blue- and white-collar workers, 1980–2006*

have not fared well in health, but women (and men) increasingly reach higher levels of education and are therefore expected to live longer.

Finally, we would like to demonstrate that developments in population health over a certain period do not necessarily look the same for all objective health measures. Figure 2.4 illustrates how another objective health measure – the proportion of overweight people, defined as having a BMI over 25 – has developed over roughly the same period.[5] At least two aspects produce different conclusions from those we observed in the above illustrations. First, the increase in the proportion of overweight people is a trend towards poorer

---

[5] BMI is calculated by dividing the weight of the person (in kilograms) by his or her weight (in metres) squared, BMI = weight in kilograms/(height in metres)^2.

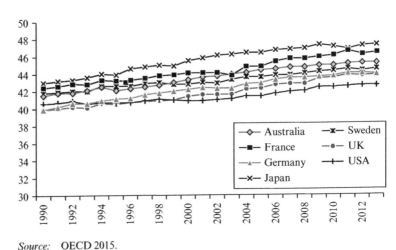

Source: OECD 2015.

Figure 2.5 *Expected remaining years of life for women at age 40*

general health, which contrasts with developments in population health such as improvements in life expectancy at age 30 over time. Second, there are no signs of an increased gap in the health of those with lower levels of education and those with higher levels of education, as indicated by the comparison above for life expectancy. If anything, there was a slight decrease in the gap in obesity between blue- and white-collar workers in the 1980s. It should be noted that the underlying data in Figure 2.4 come from surveys covering a representative but quite small share of Swedish society. The underlying data used in Figures 2.1 and 2.2, however, are drawn from public records of the entire Swedish population. Therefore, some of the observed differences in health measures may be attributed to reporting issues.

We now examine the situation in various countries in the Organisation for Economic Co-operation and Development (OECD). Figures 2.5 and 2.6 show the statistically remaining life expectancy at age 40 (shown here for men and women living in Australia, France, Germany, Japan, Sweden, the UK and the USA during the 1990–2013 period). Several interesting facts emerge from these graphs. Females tend to live longer than males, although life expectancy seems to increase for everyone over time, and the dif-

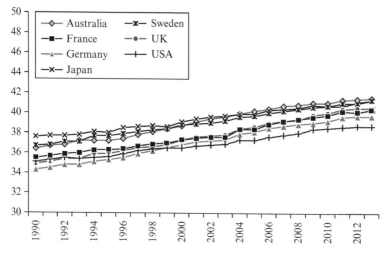

Source: OECD Health Status.

Figure 2.6   Expected remaining years of life for men at age 40

ference in life expectancy between men and women seems to shrink over time, as the gradients of the lines are steeper for men than for women. In general, these patterns appear to be uniform across countries, which highlights the importance of looking beyond country-specific phenomena to consider international developments when studying the evolution of population health.

A difficult aspect of measuring population health is that it may differ along various dimensions. The outcomes reported thus far have all indicated positive developments in health, with life expectancy rising throughout the Western world along all dimensions. Figures 2.7 and 2.8 display how another objective health measure – the proportion of overweight people as defined by having a BMI over 25 – has changed for men and women in the same seven OECD countries over roughly the same period. Recall that Figure 2.4 illustrated the same pattern in Sweden (although separately for blue- and white-collar workers).

The main message conveyed about Western health trends is now the opposite to what we noted above regarding life expectancy: Figures 2.7 and 2.8 report increasing levels in the share of overweight

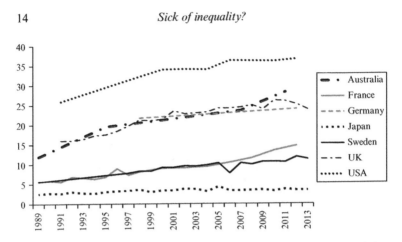

Figure 2.7   Prevalence of obesity among women – share of the adult population (15+ years)

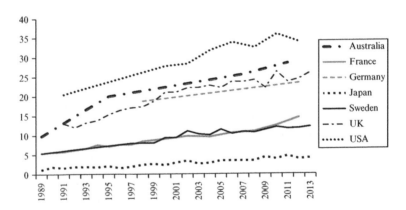

Note: Values for Sweden and France are based on self-reported data.

Source: OECD, 2015.

Figure 2.8   Prevalence of obesity among men – share of the adult population (15+)

people in the OECD, that is, that health has been deteriorating in these countries over the last years. Indeed, there is considerable variation in obesity across these seven countries, although the share of obese men and women has increased everywhere.

The purpose of these examples is to show that although objective health measures are well defined and transparent, they may generate very different views with respect to both developments in population health and distributional effects among various subgroups of the population. Measures of life expectancy indicate that population health in OECD countries has improved greatly over the last decades, whereas the share of individuals who are overweight indicates a decline over the same period. In addition, the selection of which groups to include in a study can affect the results obtained, and similarly, the results may depend on which measures are used. The health gap increases over time between some groups but decreases between others. The degree to which the level of education affects health also differs among the measures discussed above. It is therefore crucial that both scholars and laypeople understand what a specific objective health measure actually captures and remain somewhat sceptical about how individual health and population health developments are portrayed.

2.2   SUBJECTIVE HEALTH MEASURES

The main alternative to using objective health measures is to allow the individual to subjectively appraise his or her health. This can be done, for example, by rating their health on a scale from 1 (very poor) to 5 (excellent) to obtain a quantitative measure of how the individuals subjectively rate their own health.

Subjective health measures have the advantage of capturing how the individual actually feels, regardless of how objective measures say that he or she should feel. This makes it possible to measure health apart from the precise boundaries provided by the objective measures. Another advantage is that subjective measures are tied to the exact time at which the individual was asked about his or her health, whereas mortality, the most commonly used objective measure, clearly cannot be measured directly for a living population. A third advantage of self-reported assessments is that they can be collected relatively easy through non-clinical surveys of a population. Moreover, as shown by, for example, Benjamins et al. (2004) or Jylhä (2009) and the references therein, individual-level subjective measures of health often correspond well to objective measures of individual health. For example, people who claim to be in very poor health often have objective diagnoses of some sort.[6]

Nevertheless, there are several disadvantages to using subjective measures in research. The greatest shortcoming is that it is not obvious how individuals' declared subjective health statuses should be compared. What someone who is 80 years old would consider a sign of excellent health, for example, may not indicate excellent health to someone 20 years old. The minor ailments and troubles that the 80-year-old has to address – which are seen as given with advancing age – would likely be seen as very negative by a 20-year-old. Even norms about what it means to feel well can differ significantly across societal groups, countries and points in time. In some contexts and societies, it is common to find something to complain about even if people feel just fine overall. In others, people tend to exaggerate in the opposite direction. Studies show that women of all ages tend to report worse health than do men, despite the fact that women are less likely to die prematurely and less likely to become hospitalized than men. As noted by Case and Deaton (2005), this gendered pattern is almost universal.

Scholars are well-aware of these problems, and they have developed specific methods to increase the comparability of subjective health statements. Using vignettes, which are hypothetical cases of health outcomes, it is possible to correct for differences in reporting that do not result from actual differences in health between individuals and across groups (a difference referred to as reporting heterogeneity). In this method, people answer questions about their subjective health status and assess particular health issues represented in hypothetical cases (vignettes). A respondent could, for example, be asked to evaluate this hypothetical case: Anna can walk up to 200m without difficulty, but she gets tired when she walks 1km or walks up a few flights of stairs. She does not have any difficulties carrying out normal, everyday activities, such as carrying home her groceries. How would you assess Anna's mobility? For example:

---

[6] However, objective and subjective health measures are not always correlated. In a British study, subjects' answers to questions about their blood pressure were compared to their actual blood pressures, and a significant correlation between the answers given and the subject's income was observed: the lower the respondent's income, the greater their tendency to downplay problems with high blood pressure. Among those with high incomes, however, there was a near perfect correlation between subjective and objective health status (Johnston et al., 2009).

(1) none, (2) minor, (3) average, (4) good, (5) very good. Systematic differences in how respondents assess vignettes can be attributed to differences in their reporting behaviour and can thus be used to calibrate the individual's assessment of their own health. This process improves the comparability of individuals' responses.[7]

Newer studies in health economics using vignettes suggest that systematic differences in the reporting of general health status, as well as of indicators such as pain, exist by age, gender and ethnicity (Chan et al., 2011; Dowd and Todd, 2011). Furthermore, studies indicate that Europeans with high levels of education are more likely to perceive a given health status as worse than it really is; that is, in many countries, the more educated seem more likely to rate a given health state negatively. The largest differences were found in Belgium, Germany and Holland, but such reporting heterogeneity by educational groups is actually prevalent enough that there is a risk of underestimating health consequences if these differences are not considered (d'Uva et al., 2008, 2011). Based on these results, the use of vignettes is now routine in health economics. However, it is somewhat worrisome that this type of calibration is not established within epidemiological studies using self-assessed measures of health.

Figure 2.9 shows how people subjectively appraise their health in several countries. Notably, the share of respondents who answer 'bad' and 'very bad' or 'good' and 'very good' varies. In the USA and Australia, nearly 90 per cent of the population reports good health, while the corresponding figure in Japan is merely 45 per cent. These differences may mirror not only potential health differences but also cultural differences in perceptions of good or poor health. The figure thus indicates that the use of vignettes is especially important in cross-national examinations of health.

Figure 2.10 illustrates the development of subjective health in the UK and the USA for the period 2000–13. The OECD asked respondents to classify the state of their health into certain categories. The graphs indicate how the share of respondents who claimed to generally have 'good' or 'very good' health varied over time and education level.

---

[7] See Salomon et al. (2004) and Tandon et al. (2003). However, tests of the validity of vignettes have yielded contradictory results: see d'Uva et al. (2009) and Rice et al. (2010).

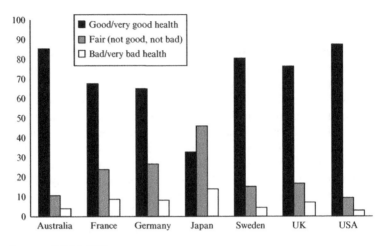

Source: OECD, 2015.

Figure 2.9   Self-assessed health status – share of adult population

Figure 2.10 clearly indicates that the majority of people in both
the UK and the USA, regardless of their education level, say that
their health is good. In both countries, the figure is significantly
higher for people with a high level of education than for people
with a low level of education, but the difference between the groups
seems to remain similar over time. That is, the trend in subjective
health seems constant. A small decline in the health-status curve of
the less educated in the UK is visible around 2011, which indicates a
possible connection between self-assessed health and economic outcomes (for example, employment). A body of literature in economics
suggests that health is pro-cyclical (Ruhm, 2000, 2005; Dehejia and
Lleras-Muney, 2004) and that population health decreases when the
economy recovers from a recession such as, for example, the 2008
financial crisis. The most common interpretation of this finding is
that good economic times have a negative impact on individuals'
health because of an increase in the opportunity cost of time, and
the resulting changes in individuals' decisions about how to allocate
their time. However, no such tendency is observed in the USA.

Another subjective measure that should be mentioned is happiness status or subjective well-being. Happiness is most commonly

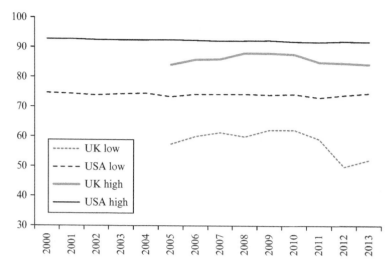

Note: Low education refers to pre-primary, primary and lower-secondary education. High education refers to tertiary education.

Source: OECD, 2015.

Figure 2.10 *Proportion of those claiming to have a good or very good general state of health*

measured in the same manner as self-assessed health; respondents are asked how happy they are, in general, on the following scale: (1) not very happy, (2) quite happy and (3) happy. A closely related measure, also used as an indicator of happiness, is responses to questions about how satisfied people are with their lives. A number of new studies in the field of happiness research have tried to capture more precisely the sense of happiness that people experience as a result of specific events, by using approaches such as the experience sampling method, in which subjects continuously report their experiences with respect to happiness and satisfaction and how powerful these experiences are perceived to be, using a handheld computer carried by the subject throughout the day. The day reconstruction method is similar in that the subject is asked to account for various events that occurred during the day at the end of each day. Contrary to more traditional ways of measuring happiness, these more sophisticated methods are believed to be able to capture other aspects of subjective well-being and to be able to establish the emotional components of happiness (for a discussion, see Knabe et al., 2010). Over the last decade, numerous studies in economics have addressed the question of what determines happiness. One observation that is relevant in this context is that health status, often measured subjectively, is generally seen as an important determinant of happiness.

2.3   THE RELATIONSHIP BETWEEN OBJECTIVE AND SUBJECTIVE MEASURES OF HEALTH

What is the relationship between the objective and subjective health measures? Are they similar in nature, simply highlighting different aspects of the same underlying health condition, or are there important differences between measures that must be kept in mind when studying their associations with economic inequality? These are broad and difficult questions to which the existing research has not provided conclusive answers. It is beyond the scope of this book to fully address this issue, but we will nevertheless consider it through a few examples.

Consider the health trends depicted in Figures 2.1, 2.2 (objective health) and 2.10 (subjective health). An interesting pattern arises: objective health (here, life expectancy) has clearly improved over time while subjective health has remained the same. Of course, it is unsatisfying that these health measures, which are commonly used by academics, show different patterns over time. There may, however, be natural explanations for these discrepancies. For example, these measures originate from different studies whose sampling or data collection methods may explain some or all of a disparity. Another explanation is that we generally quickly adapt our expectations about what constitutes good health such that we constantly raise the bar for what it means to feel good. This tendency would suggest that alternative measures really do capture different things. A third explanation is that some other factor, such as the increased prevalence of obesity seen in Figures 2.7 and 2.8, or something entirely different such as income inequality within society, counteracts the positive effects of a longer life expectancy. These explanations remain speculative. The only thing we can say with certainty, based on the above descriptive statistics, is that different health measures reveal different developments.

To sum up, this chapter shows that although it is possible to measure health quantitatively, there are many different measures – both objective and subjective – that capture relevant aspects of health. Choosing how to measure health requires great care and also that the framing of the study research question be kept in mind. Since health is multidimensional, a general conclusion that can be drawn from this chapter is that using several different measures is preferable to using just one.

3. Measuring inequality

Economic inequality, like health status, is a multifaceted concept. Inequality can be seen in terms of economic *outcomes* – for example, differences in income or wealth – or in terms of the *possibilities* that people have to influence their own lives in order to obtain the outcomes they desire. Both these dimensions are relevant and they are also intertwined, not only because differences in possibilities influence outcomes later in life but because differences in outcomes can, in turn, affect possibilities. For example, initial resources are often required to obtain an education or start a business. Most studies of health and inequality focus on inequality in outcomes, as these are easier to measure and interpret than measuring the equality of the distribution of life opportunities, which is much more difficult to measure and its relation to various health outcomes is less obvious.

Economist and philosopher Amartya Sen has claimed that, strictly speaking, equality is an aspect of distribution (Sen, 1992). To measure equality, we must not only decide which distribution should be measured but also identify an adequate way to describe the characteristics of that distribution. The distribution of annual disposable income earned by households is among the most common examined by scholars. This particular income distribution is often measured statistically using the Gini coefficient, which is a demarcated and well-defined statistical measure of the concentration of income. In many cases, the annual disposable income and Gini coefficient are based on well-established theory and practice and are considered highly adequate benchmarks, but they are by no means the only measures or even the most suitable. Many years of research on distributional issues in a variety of disciplines have produced multiple conceptual and methodological approaches.

In this chapter, we discuss the measurement of inequality by describing some of the ways that distributions can be analysed. It is important to be thorough when studying how a country's income distribution develops over time. This is even more true when trying to link inequality to social phenomena such as health, the premise of this book. Our point of departure is a set of crucial questions on which every scholar must take a position when measuring equality:[1]

- Should the equality measure be based on income or another outcome?
- If income is measured, should the measure consider taxes, welfare allowances and household structure?
- Over what time frame should inequality be measured?
- Should we measure inequality between individuals, between households or between other groups?
- Which measures are to be used to quantify inequality?

3.1 INCOME INEQUALITY OR OTHER METRICS?

A person's income is a good indicator of their material preconditions, and the simple fact that different people earn different incomes is a form of inequality that is important to measure. What makes income attractive as a measure of welfare is that it captures individuals' returns on their varying endowments in terms of ability, training and personal wealth and reflects the individual's opportunity to consume. Having said this, income is not equivalent to welfare, nor is it obvious that income differences are always the best way to capture inequality. For example, a given level of income can be associated with widely differing levels of consumption. On the one hand, if a significant part of income is saved, then consumption is lower than what income would suggest. Being in debt, on the other hand, makes it possible to consume more than current income allows for, but because the debts have to be repaid at some point in the future, consumption will need to be reduced below that period's income. Furthermore, as income can vary considerably over time – for example, from being unemployed or taking time off to have a baby – it is not necessarily representative of that person's economic status at any point in time.

---

[1] For a more in-depth discussion of how economic inequality can and should be measured see, for example, Sen (1992), Cowell (2011) and Jenkins and Van Kerm (2011).

An alternative to measuring income that is sometimes used in studies is the actual *consumption* of individuals. Patterns of consumption reveal how economic resources influence household behaviour and status. In many ways, consumption is a more stable measure than income because household consumption patterns are rarely affected by temporary changes in income. For example, after a job loss, money can be borrowed from friends and family. Conversely, a large increase in income (such as after selling a house) tends to be directed into various forms of savings rather than into immediate consumption. Some scholars argue that consumption is thus preferable as a measure as it provides a more stable measurement of prosperity (Slesnick, 2001). There are, however, problems with using consumption to measure prosperity. Most people find satisfaction in having time off and, as we grow richer, most people want to enjoy both more leisure time and more material consumption. Leisure activities, however, are not reflected in the usual measurements of material consumption. As Sen (1992) has noted, it is difficult to use consumption figures to differentiate between rich people who are fasting of their own free will and poor people who are starving. In addition to these basic objections, there is also the practical problem that in most rich countries, the available data on household consumption is typically of significantly lower quality than data on income. Household consumption is typically measured over a brief period of perhaps a few weeks, and these surveys tend to be plagued by low response rates, aggravating the problem of small samples, which make consumption data less representative of the overall population.[2]

Tax-financed services provided by the public sector pose a different kind of measurement problem, regardless of whether we measure income or consumption. For instance, in many industrialized countries families with children receive free health care for their children in addition to subsidized day care. These services are usually more important, relatively speaking, for households in lower income brackets. Paulus, Sutherland and Tsakloglou (2010) show that tax-financed services, such as day care and health care, would increase household income by approximately 25 per cent if they were to be valued and counted as a household income, decreasing inequal-

---

[2]   In poor countries it is usually the other way around – data on household consumption is often better than data on household income.

ity (that is, the Gini coefficient) by 20 per cent and cutting poverty in half. Similar results are observed in a Norwegian study of locally produced welfare services (Aaberge et al., 2010). When it comes to the distribution of welfare among households, the availability of public consumption – such as education, health care and libraries – can have a large impact on the assessed outcomes. Importantly, receiving subsidized childcare, valued at approximately €8,000 per year, for example, is not the same as receiving €8,000 in cash, which you could use for consumption in any way you see fit. Hence, there is no easy way to quantify publicly funded consumption.

Finally, it is possible to broaden the perspective of inequality beyond flows of income and consumption to focus on other dimensions, such as occupation or social class. These concepts are more or less accepted within the field of sociology, wherein scholars have developed precise schemata for occupation and class, based on an individual's position in the labour market. These classifications differentiate between employees and self-employed workers, between high and low levels of education and between supervisors and subordinates. Some concepts of class focus on the level of personal influence on the work being done, which de-emphasizes formal titles and pays more attention to the work being performed (for an overview, see, for example, Tåhlin, 2007). It is beyond the scope of this book to focus on differences in class, but class-related measurement approaches are sometimes used in epidemiological research, applying socioeconomic categories as measurements of status. We are not aware of any systematic scientific comparison of the health effects of class inequality versus income inequality, but such an analysis would certainly be valuable.

3.2   WHICH INCOME MEASURE?

Settling on income as the main outcome upon which the inequality assessment is to be based, the next step is to decide which income measure to use. As mentioned above, income can be measured in many different ways, and the choice matters for the observed level and structure of inequality. So-called *factor incomes* consist of salaries and capital income before direct taxes and transfer incomes, while *disposable incomes* are obtained by subtracting direct taxes paid (typically on income and property) from factor income and then adding transfers, such as child allowances and employment benefits. The distribution of factor income is of interest because it reflects how labour and capital market returns are distributed among households and individuals, but scholars are usually most interested in capturing the *consumption possibilities* of households, as this measure provides information on people's actual living conditions. For this reason, most scholars tend to focus on differences in disposable income when analysing income inequality.

When statistics on income distribution are presented, they are usually adjusted to reflect differences in the size and composition of households using a so-called *equivalence scale*, which facilitates the comparison of the living standards of households that are quite different. People who live together usually share some expenses (such as appliances, electronics and transportation), implying that two people who both earn incomes and share a household have a higher standard of living than they would have if they lived separately. Households with children have more mouths to feed, which is also accounted for by equivalence scales.

Adjusting for the number and age of the household members produces a measure called *equivalized disposable income* (also referred to as *disposable income per consumption unit*). In practice, this means that the incomes of people living together are multiplied by a certain factor – using the equivalence scale – compared to if they lived alone. The incomes of households with children are adjusted by another factor because children have to be provided for and are therefore counted as a burden to the household. There are a number of ways of correcting for this burden. The traditional scale used by the OECD assigns a weight of 1 to the household head (the person with the highest income), 0.7 to the second adult in the household and 0.5 to each child. This scale is being replaced by a new scale assigning weights of 1 and 0.5 to the primary and secondary income-earning adults, respectively, and 0.3 to each child.[3] Meticulous equivalence scales also consider the ages of the children in the household. For example, the scale used by Statistics Sweden assigns the same household a lower income per consumption unit if the children are aged 11–17 than if they are younger than three, as older children are seen as greater burdens in monetary terms.

---

[3]   An increasingly popular approach is to use a square-root scale, which divides household income by the square root of household size.

To illustrate the difference between the household and the individual perspectives, imagine a 20-year-old student still living with his or her parents. In a household, he or she is counted as 0.6 of a person and therefore reduces the disposable income of the household, albeit by less than if they were counted as an adult. However, this student would (most likely) be counted as poor in a population of individuals.

So far, we have identified three different income distributions that can be used to measure economic inequality: factor income, disposable income and disposable income per consumption unit (that is, disposable income adjusted for the composition of the household). Of these three, factor income (also referred to as gross income) is the most dispersed distribution, whereas disposable income (also referred to as net income) per unit of consumption is the most compressed distribution.

Which of these measures should be used to examine the effects of inequality on health? There is no single correct answer to this question. Rather, the answer depends on the mechanisms that one believes drive a relationship. If one believes that differences in actual prosperity are what matter for people's health, then disposable incomes should be used. If, however, the focus is on differences in the ability to sustain oneself, then the factor income distribution is probably a more appropriate measure. The distribution of disposable income has been by far the most commonly used income measure in inequality studies. As we noted above, this is most likely because scholars have deemed this measure to best reflect the actual level of personal welfare by capturing current consumption opportunities.

3.3 INEQUALITY OVER WHICH TIME FRAME?

Another aspect to consider when measuring inequality is the time frame over which income differences are to be evaluated. Most commonly, scholars use the distribution of annual income. This is the case in studies of the income distribution in general as well as of its relation to health in particular. There is a practical explanation for the decision to use annual incomes, namely, that income data is gathered from administrative tax records, which are typically collected on an annual basis.

However, the use of annual income to measure inequality has both advantages and disadvantages. The annual distribution of income is easy to measure and comprehend, in addition to being easy to correlate with other annual data. Furthermore, a year is a long-enough period to be less sensitive to short-term variations or lapses in income. However, it is still not certain that annual incomes capture all relevant dimensions in this respect. For example, a person having a relatively low annual income may not necessarily continue to have such a low income for a long time. In the case of a student, for example, it takes several years to obtain a college degree and, during that time, students usually earn low annual incomes, even though they will make a much better living for most of their lives. The same kind of problem occurs when people earn temporarily low incomes due to long trips, having children or unemployment.

An alternative to using annual incomes is to measure individual income over a longer period, such as over several years or even whole life cycles. Such outcomes would be less sensitive to temporary highs or lows and may better reflect stable, deeper income differences in the population. Unfortunately, it is very rare to gain access to data that allows for lifetime income calculations. Over the last few years, scholars have taken advantage of the opportunities given by some data sets to follow individuals and households over time, which has made possible the calculation of average incomes over a number of years. Typically, inequalities in lifetime incomes are smaller than in annual incomes because large decreases (such as from unemployment) or increases (such as from capital gains) in income are short-term (Björklund, 1993; Creedy, 1999; Bengtsson et al., 2016). As shown by Björklund and Jäntti (2011), however, the inequality rankings of countries are not significantly affected by shifting the analysis from annual to lifetime incomes.

3.4   INEQUALITY BETWEEN HOUSEHOLDS OR INDIVIDUALS?

The next step in preparing an analysis of the income distribution is to decide whether to study the incomes of individuals or households. The fundamental question is whether everyone in a household can be said to enjoy the same standard of living. The use of equivalence scales such as those discussed above implicitly assumes that the household's resources are distributed evenly among all of its members. However, this is partly an empirical issue: it is possible that everyone enjoys the same or similar standard of living, but the person with the highest income in a household may not distribute these resources evenly among the other members of the household.

It is clear that most previous studies of income distributions and of the relationship between inequality and health are based on households rather than individuals. The major reason is that scholars argue that equivalized household incomes better capture the true level of welfare of all individuals, essentially for the reasons described above. Focusing on individuals is nevertheless advantageous in some analyses, especially if attention is directed towards understanding success in labour or capital markets in which individual efforts and accomplishments are central. Additionally, incomes and taxes are connected to individual activities in many countries. Transfers, however, may create problems for individually based distributions because we do not know how transfer income is distributed within a household. Child allowances, for instance, are usually paid to the mother regardless of whether they are divided within the household or transferred directly to the child.

3.5 WHICH STATISTICAL MEASURE OF INEQUALITY SHOULD BE USED?

We have now discussed at length which type of inequality should be analysed, between whom and over which time frame. This leaves us with one more crucial decision to make before it is possible to examine inequality and its relation to health, namely, we must answer the following question: which statistical measure of inequality should be used? Scholars have worked for a long time to formulate principles for measuring and evaluating income inequalities within a country (see, for example, the overviews in Atkinson, 1975; Cowell, 2011). Many unidimensional measures point in the same direction, but there are still situations when measures vary and even offer different answers to questions such as what is meant by a 'more equal' distribution.

Of all statistical inequality measures, the Gini coefficient is the most well-known. The Gini coefficient takes a value between 0 and 1, where 0 indicates a perfectly even distribution in which everyone has the same income and 1 indicates that a single individual (or household) is in possession of all the income. From a strictly mathematical perspective, the Gini coefficient is a metric showing the average absolute difference in income in the population rescaled from 0 to 1. Its popularity stems not only from the fact that it is a transparent and easily interpreted ranked-based measure of inequality, but also from its solid theoretical link to several tractable tools used to characterize both distributions and their associations with normative welfare theories. Specifically, the Gini coefficient can be expressed graphically as Lorenz curves, which show the cumulative distribution function of income earners ranked by the size and relative share of their respective incomes (see, for example, Cowell, 2011).

There are, however, other ways of measuring inequality. Some of these are more technical – such as the Theil index, which relies on information theory to rank people in the population – while other measures are quite simple. A purely statistical measurement is the coefficient of variation, which is the standard deviation divided by the population mean. One family of measures produces ratios comparing the incomes of richer and poorer groups in the distribution. For example, the Q4/Q1 ratio compares the sum of the incomes of the top 25 per cent (the top quartile) to the sum of the bottom 25 per cent (the bottom quartile). One can use ratios of incomes earned at different levels of the income distribution, for example between those at the ninetieth income percentile and the median income (at the fiftieth percentile) or between the median and the tenth income percentile.

Recently, a new income inequality database documenting the evolution of top income shares over time in a number of countries was developed by a group of researchers. This data is available in the World Wealth and Income Database. A top income share is simply the share of all income that is earned by a specific group at the top of the distribution, such as the top decile or the top percentile. As most countries, until the post-war period, obliged only the richest people rather than the majority to file personal tax returns, the longest time series exist only for the very top of the income distribution. A major advantage of analysing these top income shares is thus that they are all based on homogenous source material, annual national tax returns, and on statistical methods specifically aimed to create comparability over time for each country. However, maintaining comparability of top income share data across countries is more difficult due to discrepancies in the definition of taxable income, the tax unit or the routines for collecting and reporting data. Some have ques-

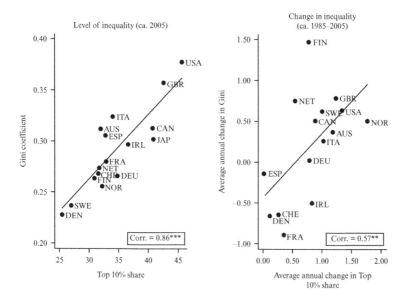

Figure 3.1   How similar are Gini coefficients and top income shares?

tioned whether top income shares are in fact appropriate measures of
inequality, as they do not fully meet all the requirements formulated
by income distribution researchers.[4] Roine and Waldenström (2015)
discuss this issue and refer to evidence of a considerable empirical
congruence between top income shares and broader measures of
income inequality. Figure 3.1 illustrates the correlation between
the Gini coefficient and the top decile share for developed countries
around 2005 and the correlation for changes in both measures over
the 1985–2005 period. Clearly, these two inequality measures are
highly correlated. Changes over a 20-year period reveal much more
variation. Between 1985 and 2005, the top decile share increased for
all countries but the Gini coefficients did not. Apparently, the extent
to which increasing inequality also implies increasing top incomes
varies substantially across countries.

---

[4]   One criterion is that transfers from richer to poorer persons should always lead to
inequality reductions. Top shares do not satisfy this criterion whenever such transfers
are made within top or bottom groups. However, when transfers are made from
someone in the top to someone in the bottom, the top shares will decrease along with
overall inequality.

Table 3.1   Four different income distributions

	Gini	CV	Top 25%	Q4/Q1	50/50
1.					
----A----B----C----D----	0.25	0.52	40%	4	2.3
2.					
----A------BC------D----	0.23	0.49	34%	4	1.9
3.					
-------A--B--C--D-------	0.15	0.31	40%	2.1	1.6
4.					
-------A---------BCD----	0.14	0.34	31%	2.5	1.5

A measure designed to capture exclusively changes at the extremes of a distribution does not, of course, provide indications about occurrences in the middle of the income distribution. A shares-based alternative to the top income shares might therefore be the 50/50 ratio, that is, the average of the upper half of the income distribution and the lower half.

How do alternative statistical inequality measures compare when applied to the same distribution? In Table 3.1, four distributions are presented. In this context, it is not important whether the scale measures annual or lifetime income, nor is it important whether the distribution refers to households or individuals. For the sake of simplicity, however, let us assume that the table refers to the distribution among four individuals: A, B, C and D. In distribution 1, individual A has the lowest income and D the highest, whereas B and C are in between. In distribution 2, the incomes of B and C are closer together than in distribution 1 but farther from A and D. According to the Gini coefficient, distribution 2 is more even than distribution 1, and we obtain the same result if we compare coefficients of variation for these distributions. The ratio of the incomes of A and D, however, is not different.

Distribution 3 is more even than distributions 1 and 2 according to all inequality measures. The comparison of distributions 3 and 4 is less obvious and, in this comparison, different measures yield different results: the Gini coefficient, the top quartile share and the 50/50 ratio indicate that distribution 3 is somewhat more unequal, whereas the coefficient of variation and the quartile ratio suggest the opposite.

A good inequality measure should be able to rank the four

distributions above – and all other possible distributions – from the least to the most equal. As seen in this example, different inequality measures can produce different rankings, and hence, determining which of two distributions is the most equal is often a matter of judgement.

3.6 ASSESSING INEQUALITY DIFFERENCES WITHIN AND ACROSS COUNTRIES

When empirically assessing an income distribution, the level of geographical aggregation needs to be determined. If inequality at the national level is relevant to population health, then international comparisons are crucial. Data is usually collected from the World Bank, OECD and the United Nations University World Institute for Development Economics Research (UNU-WIDER) databases.[5] It is, however, important to choose the same type of Gini coefficients for all countries. As taxes and welfare allowances redistribute income, Gini coefficients for gross income are usually higher than for net incomes, and it is not possible to compare coefficients calculated using gross income in one country to those using net income in another. Likewise, for most countries, data is household-based and cannot be compared with individual incomes without further calculations.

Furthermore, income distribution statistics for poor countries are often based on consumption or expenditure rather than on income. As shown by Atkinson and Brandolini (2001), these differences result in significant shortcomings when comparing inequality across countries. These differences, if not considered, can influence the observed correlations between the income distribution and various phenomena in societies.

The cross-country comparability of international income data has improved in recent years as new databases have been created to facilitate cross-national comparative studies of equality. For example, the Luxembourg Income Study (LIS) Data Center provides micro-level data for 27 countries for several years (regrettably, not annually) since the early 1980s. Figure 3.2 presents the Gini coefficients for disposable income (multiplied by 100) for six countries. To the far

---

[5]   One of the first, and best known, is the Deininger and Squire database (1996).

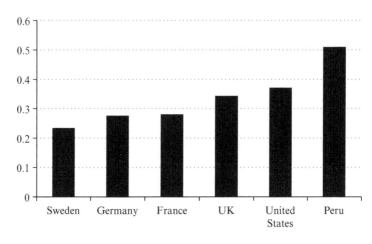

Source: Luxembourg Income Study.

Figure 3.2   Gini coefficients for disposable income in six countries around 2005

left, Sweden has relatively low Gini values between 20 and 30. The USA is significantly more unequal than the Scandinavian countries, but the highest Gini coefficients are seen in poor countries wherein a small elite often receives a large share of income.

Other surveys examine the living conditions of citizens at the European Union (EU) level, such as the European Union Statistics on Income and Living Conditions (EU-SILC). These are used in country-based comparative studies of the relationship between inequality and health. Although these databases also have their limitations, they clearly represent improvements in terms of data.

Another natural point of departure for analysing national developments is to analyse trends over time, as we did for health outcomes in Chapter 2. Unfortunately, longitudinal sources of data with adequate comparability and relatively high frequency (yearly) for a large number of countries are scarce. One notable exception is the above-mentioned World Wealth and Income Database, which provides annual top income shares data, albeit with some gaps, for approximately two dozen countries over most of the twentieth century and, for some countries, since the nineteenth century. Figure 3.3 illustrates the evolution of the top percentile income share

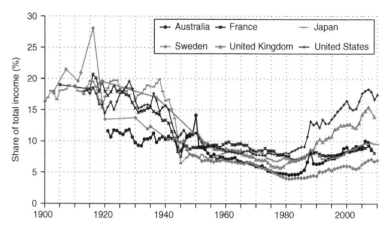

Source: WID (www.wid.world) and Roine and Waldenström (2015).

Figure 3.3 *Top income shares*

in some of these countries. Leigh and Jencks (2007) use this top income data together with long-run cross-country data on mortality to examine the long-run link between inequality and health (finding only weak evidence of such a link).

Within-country differences in income inequality can also offer important insights into the relationship between inequality and health.[6] Sweden, as we saw above, has a low Gini coefficient by international standards, approximately two-thirds of the level in the USA. However, when looking at regions within these countries, it becomes clear that there is considerable variation within both Sweden and the USA. Figure 3.4 shows the Swedish municipalities and US counties with the highest and lowest Gini coefficients for disposable annual income. On the one hand, the most equal municipality, Arvidsjaur, has a distribution of income comparable to that of the countries with the lowest level of inequality in the world, Sweden and Denmark (see Figure 3.1). The income distribution of the most unequal Swedish municipality, Danderyd, on the other hand, is more unequal than most US counties and developing countries such as Peru.

There may be multiple reasons for differences in regional inequality

---

[6] See, for instance, the analysis of Swedish municipalities by Gerdtham and Johannesson (2004).

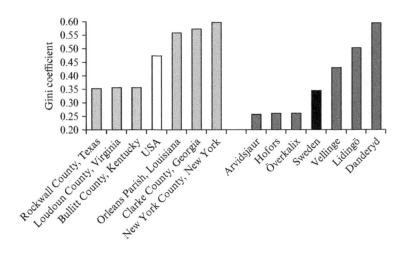

Source: US: American Community Survey (factfinder.census.gov), Sweden: Statistics Sweden.

Figure 3.4   *Gini coefficients for disposable income in the most and least equal municipalities in Sweden and counties in the United States, 2011*

in a country, and the way they interact with health outcomes can be even more complex. To begin with, looking at the most unequal US counties in Figure 3.4 suggests considerable heterogeneity, with two counties being located in relatively poor southern states (Georgia and Louisiana), while the third is the relatively well-off New York County. In addition, the three most equal counties are located in different states, which indicates that a closer look at the factors that account for these outcomes is necessary.

Sweden displays a similar pattern. The most unequal municipalities are the affluent Stockholm suburbs Lidingö and Danderyd, and the municipality of Vellinge in the southern Swedish countryside, while the most equal are in the north-eastern part of the country. Several circumstances can significantly affect the relation between inequality and health. For instance, the most equal municipalities are also the poorest, which raises the question of whether being poor in relatively equal Arvidsjaur or rich in unequal Danderyd is better for your health. This question is further complicated by the fact that the inequality of Swedish municipalities and US counties is dependent on individual choices, such as moving from poorer to richer regions. This pattern can also be considered evidence that the municipality and county are too small to capture relevant differences, which in these cases manifest at the national level. Many scholars (for example, Lundberg et al., 2010) have argued that the geographic level of aggregation affects the relationship between inequality and health, and that the mechanisms that affect the national level are different than those that matter at more local levels such as the city block.

4.   How can economic inequality influence health?

When exploring whether income differences cause bad health, one ought to have an idea of the mechanisms that might drive this relationship. Not doing so might lead to erroneous conclusions about which factors are relatively important and which are relatively unimportant or, naturally, whether an empirical correlation even exists. Determining whether economic inequality develops into health problems is no less important from a policy perspective. The lessons from the research on these links, as well as the mechanisms underlying them, can offer useful insights into the results of economic policy.

Figure 4.1 outlines possible connections among income, income inequality and health.[1] First, an individual's own income is likely to affect their health. Someone who has more money can afford better food and housing, can prevent health problems to a greater extent, such as having the resources to go to the gym regularly, and can avoid postponing doctor's visits due to limited resources. When an individual becomes richer, their health should consequently improve. This relationship is indicated by arrow 1 in the figure. Likewise, someone in good health is better able to work hard and for long hours than someone who is ill, thus earning more money and advancing their career. Hence, the opposite relationship is also likely – a person's health is affected by his or her income. This effect is indicated by arrow 2 in the figure.

When a person's income increases, however, the income distribution of the society in which the individual lives is altered. This is shown by arrow 3 in the figure. The effect is marginal when society consists of many individuals but could, of course, be significant if many individuals experience income changes at the same time. If, for instance, the income of someone who is poor increases, then the level

---

[1]   See Deaton (2003) and O'Donnell et al. (2014) for insightful discussions of these relationships.

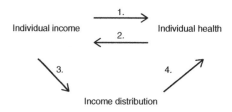

*Figure 4.1   The relationships among individual income, individual
health and societal income distribution*

of income inequality decreases according to most measures. If the
improvement occurs for someone who is already rich, then income
inequality increases. Arrow 4 in the figure captures the inequality
effect whereby the distribution of income in society influences individual health. However, why would such an effect exist? What are
the mechanisms? These questions will be examined in this chapter.

4.1   FIVE POSSIBLE MECHANISMS BEHIND
THE INEQUALITY EFFECT

Previous research – which actually occurs in a variety of scientific
disciplines – provides several theories of what might generate an
effect of inequality on health (arrow 4 in Figure 4.1). These can be
summarized as five channels:

- *Social comparisons.* People tend to compare themselves with
  others, and when income differences within a society are large,
  these comparisons lead to social stress and poorer health at the
  individual level.
- *Lower trust.* Inequality can decrease general trust, strengthen-
  ing individualism at the expense of social cohesion and public
  health.
- *Political mechanisms.* Unequal societies may neglect invest-
  ments in areas that benefit health, such as health care and
  education, and adopt policies that generally favour individuals
  with high incomes.
- *Violence and crime.* In unequal societies, individuals with low
  incomes have more to gain from stealing from those with
  higher incomes. In addition to the direct health consequences

of violence, it is also likely that, for the very same reason, people in unequal societies are more worried about violence.

- *Purchasing-power effects.* In societies with many high-income earners, goods and services that are consumed mainly by low-income earners may be more expensive or not available at all, reducing the purchasing power of the poor.

There is no consensus about these suggested mechanisms, and not all of the mechanisms suggested in the literature imply that inequality will lead to adverse health effects across the entire income distribution. For example, political mechanisms and purchasing-power effects suggest that the health of the poor may suffer because of income inequality but that high-income earners may actually benefit. Several mechanisms may also operate differently in response to both local and national income inequality.

Different scholars emphasize different mechanisms, and there is disagreement about which of these are most important. This lack of agreement largely stems from the fact that research on the possible mechanisms that mediate the relationship between inequality and health is quite recent and ongoing. Determining which mechanisms offers the best explanation is therefore often a question of empirical analysis. To examine what explains an income inequality effect on health, we need research in which these mechanisms are also tested. This kind of research, as we discuss further in the review in Chapter 7, is surprisingly rare.

4.1.1   Mechanism 1: Social Comparisons

People tend to compare themselves to one another. From an economic perspective, this could be translated into a societal position in monetary terms. Individuals identify their positions in a social hierarchy based on how they relate to other people on the income ladder. Few scholars today would argue that we are not influenced by social comparisons. For instance, people with lower incomes may feel embarrassed and less confident when they compare themselves to richer individuals. This is one of the main points made by Wilkinson and Pickett (2010). The realization of such a social position is also seen as stressful in that it can make people feel they are not in control of their lives (Marmot et al., 1991).

Scholars who argue that social comparisons affect people's health often refer to a vast body of literature on primate health. Subordinate female baboons, for instance, have been noted to have poorer ovary function and higher degrees of arteriosclerosis than their higher-ranking counterparts (Sapolsky et al., 1997). That subordinate baboons are stressed is an assumption based on the fact that they are targets of aggression from other baboons more often than those further up the hierarchy, are more vigilant, spend more time by themselves and have a higher level of the stress hormone cortisol in their bodies. In experimental research, studies have examined how changes in people's living conditions and how the stimulation of anger and frustration gives rise to stress, which in turn has physiological effects. Numerous studies analyse how, for example, these feelings increase blood pressure and cause irregular heartbeats (see Siegman, 1994; Williams et al., 2000). It is, nevertheless, still unclear why lack of control – and the associated stress – influences the cardiovascular system. One hypothesis is that repeated increases in blood pressure cause trauma to the blood vessels. Another possibility is that stress, which disrupts the normal heart rhythm, produces blood vessel spasms – in turn negatively affecting blood pressure.

Thus, one way that income inequality may negatively influence health is through social comparisons that cause stress. It is not clear, however, to which groups people tend to compare themselves. Do income differences within society matter, or do we primarily compare ourselves with people who are our same age, who do the same kind of work, who are at our workplaces, who live in our neighbourhoods or who are our closest friends? The problem of which reference group is relevant has not been solved, and theory is silent on this matter, which makes it difficult to know which type of inequality – between whom – should be measured (Deaton, 2003).[2]

It is thus reasonable to assume that the greater the inequalities that exist in a society, the more aware people are of their social positions. As we have seen, this awareness can in turn result in psychological stress, which may ultimately cause physical health problems. However, British sociologist John Goldthorpe argues that social comparisons also can be stressful – or even more stressful – in societies that are more equal. This would be the case if the concept of status includes dimensions other than income, such

---

[2]   For a discussion of the identification of reference groups, see Deaton (2003).

as having an interesting job with flexible hours (Goldthorpe, 2010). Alternatively, in some situations inequality may be associated with lower stress and therefore increased well-being. Economist Albert O. Hirschman describes a situation in which an individual who is stuck in traffic sees that the cars in the other lanes start to move ahead. If the movement of others is interpreted as a signal that the lane in which the driver is stuck will soon start to advance, then this inequality could actually increase the well-being of this person (Hirschman, 1973). In another example, a neighbour's pay rise might increase my well-being if my interpretation is 'if she can do it, so can I' or 'soon it will be my turn'. This said, if focus is on stress-causing social comparisons, then the health effect working through this mechanism ought to be negative.

4.1.2   Mechanism 2: Lower Trust

Another way that inequality can affect people's health relates to the importance of trust. A connection between high levels of income inequality and low levels of trust between people is well documented in the literature (Jordahl, 2009). A possible reason is that people do not trust one another when there are large differences in income because this inequality is interpreted as a sign that some individuals in society act dishonestly and obtain benefits at the expense of others.

The empirical correlation between income inequality and trust can also be explained by the fact that people tend to trust those who are similar to themselves; for instance, those with roughly the same income (Coleman, 1990; Fukuyama, 1995). A recent study by Bergh and Bjørnskov (2014) finds some evidence of a link between trust and income equality, suggesting that trust facilitates cooperation, the gains of which are typically divided equally among the parties involved.

How trustable people are vis-à-vis other members of society most likely influences how safe and secure they feel, which affects stress levels and health outcomes. Likewise, it is possible that trust diminishes at the expense of social cohesion, which in turn affects population health. For example, scholars argue that social networks not only have a positive effect on well-being by offering social support during stressful times, but also because these networks can be good channels for the dissemination of health-related information (Lin, 1999; Kawachi et al., 2008).

4.1.3 Mechanism 3: Political Mechanisms

A variety of political mechanisms might also explain an inequality effect on health. For instance, it might be the case that increasing inequality gives people with high incomes more power, which in turn gives them greater possibilities to influence policy such that public funds are used to benefit the rich part of the population rather than the poor. If higher incomes correspond to greater political power, it is possible that elite interests determine which political reforms are implemented – policies that in turn may influence people's health (Krugman, 1996). In this scenario, there could be cutbacks in benefits or government programmes, tax reductions or reprioritizations of the public health system in ways that harm the poor, which would also reduce average health. For example, both Araujo et al. (2008) and Deaton (2013) suggest that inequality relates to the allocation of health-related public goods, such as immunizations, and the provision of subsidized medical care, which in turn implies that children growing up during periods of greater income inequality will receive fewer health inputs.

Even when a political situation is more democratic, there is reason to believe that the degree of public spending on health care may be proportional to inequality, as the preferences of the rich and the poor for how public money should be used vary widely in unequal societies (Alesina et al., 1999). If high inequality generates a low level of confidence in government institutions – in particular, if the public believes that those representing these institutions are growing richer – then inequality may also generate a situation in which people increasingly refrain from voting in elections (Brehm and Rahn, 1997). The consequence of such a development might include that the needs of non-voters are largely neglected, which in turn could affect population health.

4.1.4 Mechanism 4: Violence and Crime

A fourth mechanism by which economic inequality might affect health relates to the fact that societies with large income differences often experience problems with violence and crime. Crime may be more common in economically unequal societies because people feel that their disadvantaged economic situation is permanent. They cannot obtain the material attributes that symbolize success, which may generate feelings of frustration, powerlessness and alienation. Such alienation may break down societal values, such as kinship and affinity, over time and lead to higher crime rates (Merton, 1968). Economic theory also predicts a positive relationship between economic inequality and the rate of property crime. This prediction is based on the assumption that, given a risk of being caught, large income differences increase the expected return of crime relative to legal activities (Becker, 1968; Ehrlich, 1973). Besides the direct influence of a high crime rate on the well-being of victims, fear of crime – affecting oneself or one's friends and family – may also negatively affect how people feel psychologically and physically (Green et al., 2002; Di Tella and MacCulland, 2008).

4.1.5   Mechanism 5: Purchasing-Power Effects

A fifth mechanism, which is not typically discussed in the inequality and health literature, concerns the relationship between income inequality and inequality of purchasing power. As noted by Pendakur (2002), the nominal incomes of the rich and the poor in a country are typically deflated using the same price vector when real incomes are calculated. This approach ignores differences in both the prices and consumption patterns of high- and low-income earners. In societies with relatively more high-income earners, fewer goods and services are likely to be targeted towards the poor, and those that exist may be more expensive due to the smaller market size. However, as elaborated in Chapter 8, the implied relationship between inequality and health is ambiguous: an increase in the number of poor people may both lead to higher income inequality and increase the purchasing power of the poor.

4.2   IS ALL INEQUALITY BAD?

Although there are many arguments for why a negative relationship between inequality and health might exist, some mechanisms actually indicate that income differences could have positive effects both on the economy and on individual health. In market economies, variation in prices and earnings plays an important role in information sharing and resource allocation. The high earnings of certain professions indicate high labour-market demand for this group, which, in turn, simply reflects the fact that this group offers something that others are willing to pay for. As these high salaries attract additional workers to the profession, more of this demand can be met. When a commodity or service attracts a high price relative to its production cost, this indicates that many people are willing to pay more than what it costs to make. The possibility of profits attracts more producers and increases the supply of the commodity or service. The price system thus contributes to the allocation of both labour and capital to where they are most beneficial from a societal perspective. In addition, economic efficiency should, at least over the long term, be beneficial to health. From a purely economic perspective, it is therefore likely that the economy works better if there exist some income differences between groups and individuals.

If there are simultaneously positive and negative health effects of inequality, what does this relationship look like when all these effects are considered? This is a difficult and complex question to answer. Figure 4.2 shows a stylized sketch of the correlation between inequality and health; it depicts a situation in which the negative health effects caused by inequality become worse with larger income differences, which is entirely reasonable to assume. The positive health effects produced by economic efficiency, however, are dominant when the income differences between individuals are small, on average, whereas the negative health effects are dominant at high levels of inequality. If this line of reasoning is correct, then we will observe a negative association between inequality and health only when inequality reaches a threshold level.

There is extensive debate about inequality within the field of political philosophy. The question, simply put, is not whether

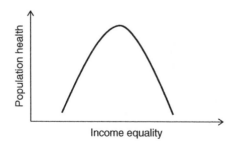

Figure 4.2   A possible correlation between income inequality and population health

inequality is desirable but what should be equally distributed (Sen, 1992). According to a common philosophical perspective, some differences, such as in income, are acceptable if they reflect peoples' deliberate choices and desires, but they are inequitable if they result from factors that are beyond the control of individuals. Naturally, where the line between free choice and circumstances that cannot be altered is located is not obvious because few choices are entirely free and few circumstances are entirely immune to alteration.[3]

In a related body of literature, behavioural studies and economics experiments suggest that people show less acceptance of inequality and income differences if these differences are seen as the result of unfairness, and are more acceptable if the income differences are considered the result of a fair procedure (see, for example, Konow, 2000). If public perception of income differences influences both social comparisons and stress, then it is reasonable to assume that the health effects of income differences depend on how these differences occurred. It is therefore quite possible that an income distribution that developed in a system characterized by discrimination – in which the same opportunities have not been available to everyone – may lead to stress, frustration and poor health. If, however, the same income distribution is produced by free elections and a fair process, then an inequality effect on health might not be observed.

4.3   SUMMING UP

In this chapter, we have presented and discussed the most important hypotheses about how income inequality can influence people's health. Too rarely do scholars and commentators take the necessary time to try to understand why people get sick or experience poorer health due to income differences. Most researchers are satisfied with merely identifying whether this is the case. However, we believe that a discussion of which underlying factors – or mechanisms – explain this assumed relationship is crucial. Exploring mechanisms matters both for producing a study whose findings are scientifically convincing and for interpreting the results to provide politicians and

---

[3]   For a more in-depth discussion, see Roemer (1996).

other stakeholders with informed recommendations about how this issue should be appropriately addressed.

The mechanisms discussed in the literature point to widely differing explanations for the observed relationship between income inequality and health: social structures, psychological phenomena, monetary factors and political processes. Some of these reasons manifest primarily at the micro level – among individuals or households – either within people or through interpersonal connections. Other mechanisms generally function at the macro level, where societal structures – that are related to the health care system, economic growth and redistribution – matter. At the end of the day, which of these mechanisms is the most important must be determined empirically.

We have here also noted that inequality may not be detrimental in all situations. There are reasons to believe, for example, that high returns to education (such as large differences based on degrees earned or years of education) may provide incentives to increase education, which would be positive for both individuals and society. Overall, the association between inequality and health might include both positive and negative components. An inverted U-shaped pattern (Figure 4.2) illustrates an inequality effect that is positive at low levels of income inequality but negative at high levels.

5. Correlation or causality? Interpreting scatter plots and regressions

The relationship between inequality at the country level, measured as the Gini coefficient for disposable income, and health measured using life expectancy at birth can be illustrated using a scatter plot such as the one in Figure 5.1. In this graph, each dot represents a country for which inequality is measured along the x-axis and life expectancy is measured along the y-axis. The straight line in the diagram indicates the best fit.[1] The line has a downward slope, which means that the global correlation between these variables is negative: a higher level of income inequality is associated with lower life expectancy.

However, if we were to look at the situation within a specific country, we might see the opposite relationship. Using data from 21 Swedish counties, Figure 5.2 shows that life expectancy is higher in counties with a higher level of income inequality. In Sweden, roughly the same picture can be seen at the municipal level. On average, municipalities with higher levels of income inequality have higher life expectancies at birth.

Looking more closely at Figure 5.2, it seems unlikely that the positive slope indicates that inequality causes better health. In the upper-right part we find rich, urban counties such as Uppsala and Stockholm, while in the bottom left we find relatively poor and rural Norrbotten. One might suspect that higher economic growth in Stockholm is related to lower unemployment, better-paying jobs and, therefore, better health. At the same time, urban economic growth in Sweden's capital also leads to high income inequality. Another possibility is that the share of people with high education

---

[1] More precisely, the plotted line uses the least squares method, which minimizes the sum of the squared vertical distance between the plots and the line.

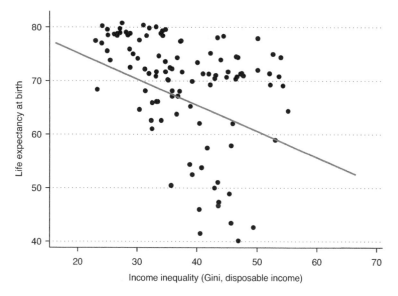

Source: Data from Bergh and Nilsson (2010).

Figure 5.1   The correlation between inequality and life expectancy across countries in 2002

varies across counties and that the highly educated have both higher incomes (explaining income inequality) and healthier life-styles (explaining life expectancy). Without actually examining these factors, however, we are only speculating.

Figure 5.3 replicates for France what Figure 5.2 shows for Sweden, and a positive correlation between income inequality and life expectancy can be seen, although it is quite weak and there is considerable variation around the fitted correlation line. Still, the pattern that could be seen within Sweden seems to appear in France as well, with relatively rich Ile-de-France (that includes Paris) in the top-right corner and relatively poor and rural Picardie in the bottom left.

Using a different measure of health changes the picture substantially. In Figure 5.4, we show the inequality–health relationship across Swedish counties using the number of new cases of cancer per 100,000 inhabitants in a year as the measure of (poor) health. The pattern appears clear: counties with higher income inequality

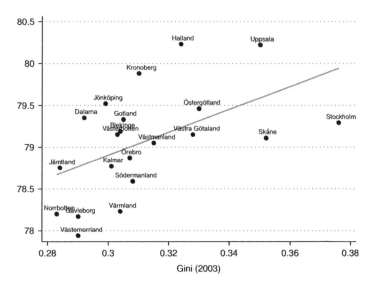

Source: Statistics Sweden (2010) and Statistics Sweden (2003).

Figure 5.2   Regional inequality and life expectancy at birth in Sweden

also have a higher incidence of cancer, that is, a negative correlation between inequality and health. However, in France (Figure 5.5) the opposite relationship to Sweden is observed! In France, the lowest numbers of cancer cases are found in the regions with the highest level of inequality.

The patterns illustrated in Figures 5.1 through 5.5 convey at least two important lessons. First, there is no clear-cut raw correlation between income inequality and health. Scatter plots can easily illustrate both positive and negative correlations between inequality and health. The geographical levels at which inequality and health are measured matter, as do the actual health measures used. Even when the measures are identical, the nature of the relationship may differ across rich democracies – as it does for Sweden and France when health is measured by the cancer incidence.

The second lesson is that statistical correlations do not inform us about causal effects. The correlations between inequality and health illustrated in Figures 5.1 and 5.4 do not provide proof that income inequality causes sickness, nor do the correlations in Figures 5.2

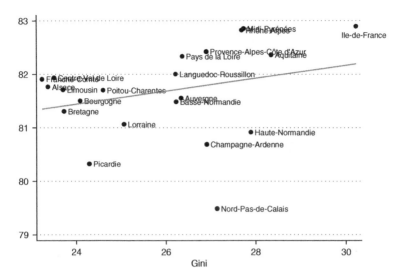

Source: France National Statistics Office, 2013.

Figure 5.3   Regional inequality and life expectancy at birth in France

and 5.5 prove the opposite. Verifying a causal relationship is much more intricate than finding statistical correlations between variables.

This chapter discusses what statistical correlations can tell us and how correlations between inequality and health may be analysed in a more thorough and sophisticated way. In the next chapter, we take a closer look at which types of data and statistics are required to determine whether we get sick as a result of income inequality.

5.1   DO HIGHER INCOMES LEAD TO BETTER HEALTH OR DOES POOR HEALTH LEAD TO LOWER INCOMES?

As discussed in Chapter 4, we expect that negative health effects stem from inequality for a number of reasons (such as social comparisons, violence, policy effects). However, it is also possible that poor health among some individuals in the population causes a high level of inequality. For example, this could be the case when individuals are too sick to work and therefore make less money than others.

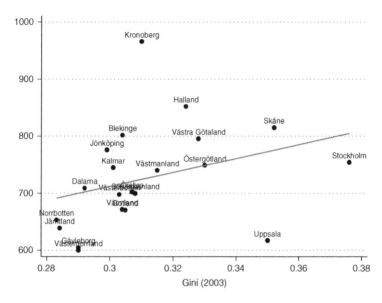

Source: Statistics Sweden (2011) and the Swedish National Board of Health and
Welfare (2011).

*Figure 5.4   Regional inequality and the number of new cases of
cancer in Sweden (per 100000 inhabitants)*

Scholars often propose two mechanisms for how poor health
depresses individual incomes. The first concerns job-market effects.
People who are often ill may face difficulties entering the job market,
either because they are too sick to apply for a job or because employ-
ers become reluctant to hire people who are frequently absent. Even
when they have a job, individuals who are often sick tend to work
less, perhaps less efficiently, and may thus have less career opportunities as compared to others.[2] Overall, there are several reasons why
healthier individuals are more likely to become wealthy (Lee, 1982;
Luft, 1975). Another possibility is that people with less ability to
work due to physical or mental disabilities are discriminated against
in the job market but, for many reasons, this is much more difficult
to demonstrate empirically.

[2] Heckman (2007) provides an extensive theoretical framework for how
health affects labour supply and productivity.

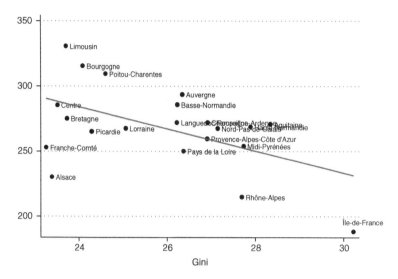

Source: France National Statistics Office, 2013.

Figure 5.5   *Regional inequality and the number of new cases of cancer in France (per 100 000 inhabitants)*

The second proposed mechanism is about education effects. In a study of children who were foetuses at the time of the nuclear accident in Chernobyl, Almond et al. (2009) find that, when fallout rained down on certain geographical areas, the exposed children later tended to have lower cognitive skills and to learn more slowly in school. Negative outcomes in the job market were also observed as these children reached maturity. Scholars therefore argue that they have found a credible link between poor health (through the effect of fallout on foetal development) and negative subsequent education and income outcomes. Poor health probably also negatively affects school performance, even among older children and adolescents, because when you are sick you are absent more and, perhaps primarily, bad health negatively influences an individual's ability to learn. Currie and Stabile (2006) find that the mental and physical health of children is linked to their ability to concentrate and learn at school. Black et al. (2007) have found a similar correlation between the birth weights of newborns in Norway and later outcomes in life, where an increase in birth weight of 10 per cent increased the possibility of graduating from high school by 1 per cent and increased income by 1 per cent.[3]

There is some disagreement across academic disciplines regarding the nature of the causal relationship between health and income. Scholars within the fields of social medicine and public health often assume that increased incomes lead to health benefits. In the economics literature, however, scholars often note that there is also a causal effect in the opposite direction and that the distribution of health may therefore influence the distribution of income.[4] A case in point occurred when health economists Canning and Bowser (2010) published a review of the *Marmot Review* – an ambitious study of the unequal distribution of health and its causes in England (Marmot, 2010). Epidemiologist Michael Marmot argues in this investigation that the unequal distribution of health is best counteracted by reducing economic inequality, while Canning and Bowser claim that the same statistics indicate that efforts should target the sickest in order to increase their ability to work and make money. In other words, Canning and Bowser argue that the poor health of some individuals primarily explains the unequal distribution of income through the job market and education mechanisms discussed above, and not the other way around.

The dispute illustrates that even prominent scholars can disagree about the nature of a causal connection even though they analyse more or less the same data and identify the same correlations. It is difficult to say who makes the best case, and there are clear indications that the causal relationship of interest is actually dual; that is, that causal mechanisms run both from health to income and from income to health. These mechanisms could also magnify each other, resulting in a vicious circle in which poor health causes inequality, which in turn exacerbates health problems.

Does the disagreement about the direction of the causal relationship mean that it is impossible to arrive at a general conclusion about this issue? We think not. Methods for analysis are constantly improved upon and become more sophisticated; new data

---

[3] Almond and Currie (2011) and Currie and Rosin-Slater (2015) are newly published surveys of the research on the long-term effects of foetal and new-born health status.
[4] Deaton (2003) argues that income and health probably influence each other, and judging by the results reported in the literature, one of the main conclusions is that income and health may be mutually determined.

is gathered, and some studies are already well on their way to more credible results. Most of these studies use the method of natural experiments. Ideally, to identify causality, you need a laboratory in which scholars can alter a single variable (for example, the distribution of income) and then study the effect on another variable (such as health). In such a laboratory, you could experiment with the salary distribution, income and all of society's taxes and transfers in a controlled manner and then see how individual health is affected. These kinds of social-science laboratories are difficult to imagine in real life (thank goodness). There are, nevertheless, laboratory-like contexts that are exciting in their own right, and these are consequently referred to as natural experiments.

In a natural experiment, natural and ideally random variation in a variable (such as health) occurs for some reason, so this variation can be used to study its effect on other factors. The effect of health on income, for example, has been analysed using variations in health created by the distribution of malaria across geographical contexts or sudden medical breakthroughs or incidents, such as the Spanish flu pandemic (Almond, 2006). Another example is the Chernobyl nuclear disaster and subsequent nuclear fallout, where the wind patterns after the accident determined the distribution of radioactivity in ways that could be foreseen by anyone. The opposite direction of causality, that is, from income to health, has been analysed using variations in income caused by lottery winnings (Lindahl, 2005; Gardner and Oswald, 2007).[5]

These studies support the hypothesis that health influences individual income as well as the hypothesis that income influences individual health.[6] Frijters et al. (2005) argue that the fall of the Berlin Wall constitutes a good natural experiment, as people in the former East Germany suddenly and unexpectedly received higher incomes. People in West Germany can be used as a control group because their incomes did not change. The authors conclude that higher

---

[5] Based on lottery winnings in Sweden, Cesarini et al. (2016) conclude that in affluent countries with extensive social safety nets, the causal effects of wealth on health are small or non-existent.

[6] Although Lindahl's (2005) results indicate a causal effect moving from income to health, there is also an effect of good health on income, as the size of the positive income effect decreases when this correlation is evaluated using an instrumental analysis.

incomes clearly have a positive (albeit quite small) effect on subjective health.[7]

There are also problems with the natural experiment approach. One is that even if the experiments allow researchers to identify causal effects, they might not generalize to policy-relevant contexts. While nuclear fallout or the fall of the Berlin Wall provide good opportunities for research, events like these are obviously not standard tools used by policy makers. Instead, tools such as health insurance policies, taxes, welfare services and regulatory frameworks must be used. It is not clear that the outcomes of two-month-old foetuses 20 years after Chernobyl, or those of the East German population after the fall of the Wall, can tell us much about the results of health-care reform in any present-day locality. Regardless of problems with generalizability (that is, the external validity of natural experiments), these results are still among the most reliable available in the social sciences today, and we believe that they should be part of an informed discussion of the existing evidence.

5.2   ADDRESSING SPURIOUS CORRELATIONS

Another challenge in establishing a causal relationship is that statistical correlations between variables may not reflect meaningful causal relationships. This can occur when a correlation emanates from a third variable influencing both variables of interest. This phenomenon is sometimes referred to as *spurious correlation*. If a factor causes certain countries or regions to be more unequal and to have worse health, a correlation like the one seen in Figure 5.1 can arise without an underlying causal relation between health and inequality. Which factors may result in such spurious correlations? A possible candidate is age distribution. It is well known that older people usually have lower levels of health compared to the rest of the population, as well as lower incomes than those who are still working. It is therefore possible that both income inequality and poor health are greater in areas with large numbers of older people. If this is the case, bad health is not caused by inequality. Instead, the correlation is

---

[7]   The item used to answer the question was 'How satisfied are you currently with your health situation?' The responses were coded on a scale from 0 (very unsatisfied) to 10 (very satisfied) (Frijters et al., 2005).

explained by a high number of older people having both low incomes and lower levels of health. In this case, age distribution is said to be an *omitted variable*.

A common method used by scholars to address omitted variables, and therefore reducing the risk of identifying spurious correlations, is to include the omitted variables in the analysis (in which case they are no longer omitted). If the correlation between inequality and health, for example, remains after controlling for the proportion of older people in the population, then that particular source of error can be ruled out. The problem is that it is often possible to imagine a great number of variables that may cause spurious correlations. If data for these variables is not available, the problem is harder to rectify.

Another way to avoid spurious correlations is to study changes over time (as in time variation) rather than differences across countries or regions (as in cross-sectional variation).[8] Suppose that we are studying inequality and health in a number of cities. These cities are similar in most respects, apart from the fact that some of them have attracted large populations of high-skilled physicians. When inequality and population health in these cities are compared, the cities with the most dispersed income distributions also have the healthiest populations. This, however, does not imply that inequality leads to improved population health. The most likely explanation is that the higher incomes of the high-skilled physicians increases inequality in these cities while the high density of physicians simultaneously improves population health. In this example, we can control for physician density by either including it in the analysis or comparing changes over time rather than levels.

This method of analysing change over time requires that a few preconditions be fulfilled. For example, the effect of having more physicians has to remain constant over time. If physician density also changes over time, then this needs to be addressed. It is also necessary that the distributions of income evolve differently in the two cities if we wish to be able to identify an inequality effect. Furthermore, it is necessary that enough time be allowed to pass for changes in the income distribution to affect people's health. It is unlikely that an inequality effect would be seen in the data if

---

[8]   This, of course, requires that the omitted variables not change much over time.

cities are only observed at two points in time that are close together. Finally, the change in the income distribution should be exogenous (that is, not explained by something already present in the analysis). The search for exogenous variation leads scholars to look for natural experiments, such as the fall of the Berlin Wall or winning the lottery, as described above.

5.3 THE IMPORTANCE OF ECONOMIC SIGNIFICANCE

A common mistake in interpreting statistical correlations is to overlook the magnitude of the effects. When determining whether a correlation is statistically significant (as in that it is possible, with a high degree of certainty, to establish that the effect is not zero) in addition to pointing in the 'right direction' (that is, whether it is positive or negative), many studies do not evaluate the size of the effect. A statistically significant correlation is an observed correlation that, with a high degree of certainty, is not the result of random variation. Saying that something is statistically significant, therefore, means that a correlation of some sort exists. It does not, however, say anything about the importance of this correlation, which requires a look at the size of the effect generally referred to as the economic significance.

It is commonplace, even among prominent scholars, to overlook the size of an effect.[9] The difference between economic and statistical significance is important, not least from a public policy perspective. If a reform is implemented to improve the health of people, then we would like to know not only how likely it is that the reform leads to improved health but also the degree of its effectiveness. The first question is a matter of statistical significance, whereas the latter refers to the magnitude of the effect. Most commonly, an effect is considered statistically significant if the probability is at least 95 per cent that it is different from zero. There is, however, no higher scientific truth saying that the limit should be 95 per cent.

---

[9] McCloskey and Ziliak (1996) refer to the overlooking of effect size and economic significance as 'sizeless science'. They note that failure to discuss effect size is common even in reputable economics journals.

Even if a significant causal correlation from inequality to individual health is identified, it is still possible that the effect is so small that it is easier and more effective to improve peoples' health through other measures that have a greater effect. Another possibility is that the correlation between inequality and health does not reach the 95 per cent level of significance usually required for it to be considered scientifically valid but that the effect nonetheless is so large compared to other policy measures that it is worth considering.

A good way to get a feel for the difference between statistical and economic significance is the following thought experiment. Imagine that you are to recommend one of two drugs to someone who is overweight. One of these drugs has a 99 per cent probability of reducing the person's weight by 0.5 kilos. The statistical significance of the effect of this drug is high, but the effect is clearly very small. The other drug has a 90 per cent probability of reducing the person's weight by 15 kilos, that is, there is a 10 per cent probability of no weight reduction. Most people would probably prefer to use the second drug but, because of the accepted 95 per cent probability or higher threshold, only the first drug can boast statistically significant weight reduction.

5.4 INTERPRETING STATISTICAL INEQUALITY EFFECTS ON HEALTH: AN EMPIRICAL EXAMPLE

We will now leave behind the hypothetical examples and instead conduct a simple quantitative analysis of actual country-level data on inequality and life expectancy, using the data in Figure 5.1 as a starting point. The purpose is to illustrate and discuss the methodological problems addressed above using actual data. As does the bulk of previous research, we use aggregate data.[10] When information on health is aggregated over individuals, so-called population health measures are generated. These reflect the general state of health of the population. In the next chapter, we discuss in greater depth some pitfalls of interpreting correlations in aggregate data.

---

[10] The term aggregate data refers to statistics collected for a certain population within a geographical area – in our case, average outcomes of entire countries and their populations.

Table 5.1   *Explaining life expectancy using inequality and other variables (aggregated data, variation between countries, 1970–2005)*

	(1)	(2)	(3)	(4)	(5)
Gini (t − 1)	−0.190***	−0.147***	−0.117***	−0.101***	−0.017
	[0.047]	[0.049]	[0.035]	[0.035]	[0.031]
Trust		0.201***		0.069*	0.050*
		[0.060]		[0.042]	[0.029]
GDP per			4.898***	4.842***	2.427***
capita			[0.429]	[0.445]	[0.503]
Physicians					3.063***
					[0.404]
Nutrition					6.938***
					[2.667]
Constant	73.501***	66.910***	29.742***	27.910***	−8.383
	[1.875]	[2.939]	[4.467]	[4.081]	[19.830]
Observations	502	502	502	502	502
Number of countries	105	105	105	105	105

Source: Own calculations based on data from Bergh and Nilsson (2010) and Berggren and Bjørnskov (2011).

5.4.1   Using Cross-Country Variation to Analyse Inequality and Health

We now examine the pure correlations shown above and determine whether they should be qualified, that is, if they depend on omitted variables. In this section, we also examine the size of the link between inequality and health to compare its relevance with that of other population health correlates. This can be done by comparing outcomes in different countries.

The first column of Table 5.1 offers a closer look at the cross-country correlation between life expectancy and income inequality measured as the Gini coefficient for annual disposable income. These are both measured as five-year averages to minimize noise and measurement error stemming from annual fluctuations.[11] Note that we

---

[11]   The regressions below are based mostly on data available from the WDI database provided by the World Bank. The database collects observations from 126 countries

use lagged inequality to address some simultaneity problems, reflecting the notion that if inequality causes poor health, then the cause should occur before the effect. However, simply lagging explanatory variables rarely suffices to address the problems of causality and establishing a causal relationship. Health and economic outcomes are likely to influence one another throughout life, as shown by, for example, Haas (2006).[12]

Beginning with the first column of Table 5.1, there is a statistically significant negative correlation, which reinforces the correlation shown in Figure 5.1. This result is consistent with the inequality hypothesis, and its statistical significance is high.[13]

Is the measured effect in column one economically important? Answering this question requires calculations based on information from the table and knowledge about the included variables. As we saw in Chapter 3, the Gini coefficient multiplied by a factor of 100 is approximately 25 for Sweden and 37 for the USA.[14] In the UK, the Gini coefficient increased from 27 to 32 during the Thatcher era.[15] The size of the estimated coefficient in column one therefore means that if inequality in a country were to increase to the same degree that it did in the UK under Thatcher, that is, approximately five units, then life expectancy would decrease by almost 1 year ($5 \cdot 0.190 = 0.95$). This is quite a large effect, but keep in mind

---

over a maximal period of 35 years (1970–2005). All observations, except the first, represent five-year averages, which means that we have data from 1970, 1971–5, 1976–80 and so on, until the 2001–5 period. Using averages over several years is a commonly used method to avoid short-term fluctuations. These fluctuations seldom provide information about the underlying correlations, but there is always the risk that they introduce some confusion into the analysis. The data used in this empirical study comes from Bergh and Nilsson (2010).

[12] A person's health during one period is a function of their health in a previous period, both directly and indirectly, through the influence that health has on income and therefore on inequality. Generally, there is no guarantee that cause precedes effect.

[13] The number of asterisks (*) in Table 5.1 is used to illustrate the degree of statistical significance and is an indicator of the probability that the negative correlation is actually random. Usually, * is used to indicate that the probability is less than 10 per cent, ** that it is less than 95 per cent and *** that it is less than 1 per cent.

[14] The inequality measurement used includes only income generated by labour. The Gini coefficient increases when capital gains are included.

[15] The fact that the level of inequality increased when Thatcher was prime minister, however, is not sufficient evidence that Thatcher (or her policies) caused this rise. For a further discussion on why inequality increased during this period, see, for instance, Clark and Leicester (2004).

that this interpretation is only correct if we have found a causal connection between the two variables and if no other factors need to be controlled for, which is highly unlikely.

In columns two, three and four in the table, we account for the possibility that countries in which social trust is high benefit from better health, higher income and perhaps more equal incomes.[16] In this case, social trust is an omitted variable that should be controlled for. Similarly, we might expect richer countries to have better health, and they tend to have lower income inequality. The columns show the results from testing the effects of social trust and gross domestic product (GDP) per capita, which both turn out to be correlated with life expectancy. When they are included, the coefficient on inequality decreases to roughly half its initial size. We also see that the large effect of social trust in column two comes mainly from the fact that countries with high social trust tend to be richer. Still, even controlling for GDP per capita, countries in which 10 per cent more respondents agree that most people can be trusted have, on average, life expectancies that are eight months longer. The 'effect' of GDP per capita on population health may reflect the fact that people in richer countries can afford to eat better and to spend more money on health.

Finally, in column five, we account for the density of physicians (measured as the number of physicians per 1,000 inhabitants) and the average intake of calories in each country and period. Both of these variables also appear to matter, and we note that when we include them, the coefficient on GDP per capita decreases by nearly one-half. What does this mean? Most likely, this pattern reflects the simple fact that a high income level is instrumentally important because it allows for the consumption of other things that are directly related to health. When these factors are explicitly included and held constant, the effect of higher GDP per capita decreases.

Most importantly, including physician density and average calorie intake diminishes the effect of inequality, and it is no longer significantly different from zero. Does this imply that the inequality hypothesis has been rejected? Not necessarily. When testing a proposed

---

[16] Note that we keep the sample constant in all columns even though there may be more observations when only some of the control variables are included. This is not always done in published research, which may affect the comparability of results across specifications.

hypothesis, we want to control for other factors that might bias the relationship. In our example, social trust and GDP per capita may be seen as factors that we need to control for because the estimate will otherwise suffer from omitted variable bias. We should not, however, control for variables that capture the hypothesized mechanisms by which inequality affects health. If our hypothesis is that politicians in more unequal countries will pursue different policies that lead to lower nutritional intake and fewer physicians, then the fact that the Gini coefficient is significant in column four but much smaller and less significant in column five is exactly what we would expect: more unequal countries have lower life expectancies, and the effect is explained by the fact that countries that are more unequal have lower intakes of calories and fewer physicians per capita. Observing these patterns does not prove that a higher density of physicians is an effect of political processes with different outcomes in equal and unequal countries, but it is consistent with that theory.

Are other theories consistent with the patterns observed? One possibility is that high physician density in a country reflects the level of education in that country and that education, rather than the number of physicians, explains why these countries have higher life expectancies. This is a reasonable assumption, but when Bergh and Nilsson (2010) included the level of education in their analysis, it was not statistically significant while physician density remained so. This suggests that the effect of physicians cannot be explained by a correlation between education and population health.

Can we somehow compare the effect of, for example, GDP per capita to the effect of inequality? Because GDP per capita is measured logarithmically, the coefficient is interpreted as follows: an increase of 10 per cent in GDP per capita is associated with an increase in life expectancy of approximately six months (based on the coefficient in column four). Is this a large or a small effect compared with the inequality effect? We can gauge these magnitudes by relating the coefficient estimates to the standard deviations of the different variables.

In Table 5.2, we have done this for three explanatory variables to compare their magnitudes. If we interpret these effects causally – which is not an obvious thing to do – then an increase in trust of one standard deviation would lead to an increase in life expectancy of approximately one year, and an increase in the Gini coefficient by one standard deviation would decrease life expectancy just as much.

*Table 5.2   Life expectancy (number of years) effects of one
standard deviation increases in three different variables
(based on column 4 in Table 5.1)*

Variable	Mean	Std. dev.	Coefficient	Effect
Gini	*37.25*	*10.35*	−0.101	−1
Trust	*26.40*	*14.93*	0.0691	1
GDP per capita (log.)	*8.46*	*1.10*	4.842	5.3

Note: Here, an increase in income inequality should be interpreted as an increase
of the Gini coefficient by one standard deviation.

These effects are by no means small, but they are dwarfed by the
effect of a one standard deviation increase in logged GDP per capita,
which would increase life expectancy by over five years. Note that
because GDP per capita is logged, the dollar amount required to
increase life expectancy by a given number of years is much lower
for countries that are poorer from the beginning. A coefficient of 4.8
means that a 10 per cent increase in GDP per capita is associated
with an increase in life expectancy of 0.48 years.

What this exercise has shown is that the size of the inequality effect
may change dramatically when accounting for other explanatory
variables. Had we used the coefficients from column five instead of
column four in Table 5.2, the Gini coefficient would not even be significant, while the effect of trust remains – although it is slightly smaller.
This underlines the importance of using theoretically motivated
models that incorporate not only inequality and health variables
but also variables that are possibly related. Which variables should
be used? There is no simple answer to this question, but there are
potentially a vast number of factors, varying from country to country,
which may have an impact on population health. Having said this, all
of these cannot be included at the same time, partly because of limited
observations and partly because we simply do not know all the relevant factors.[17] Luckily, there are statistical methods that can help in
this situation, which is the theme of the following section.

---

[17]   This is not just difficult to do practically; it is also mathematically impossible to
identify more explanatory factors than the number of observations. The number of
observations should be significantly higher than the number of independent variables
in order to obtain precise estimates.

5.4.2   Using Longitudinal Variation to Analyse Inequality and Health

Adjusting for all factors that theoretically influence inequality and health in different countries is essentially impossible. An often-used alternative is to account for all factors that, at a given point in time, influence all countries by including a so-called *time fixed effect.* Similarly, there may be country-specific factors that influence a given country at all times that can be corrected for by including a so-called *country fixed effect.* Naturally, doing so requires access to data for a number of countries over many years, which is national panel data. An example of a time fixed effect is that most countries had lower levels of average health at the start of the study period than they did at the end. An epidemic influencing all countries at a certain time would also be considered a time fixed effect. We can exclude time effects by introducing an indicator variable – a dummy variable – for each period being studied to capture the time fixed effects of that period.[18]

Table 5.3 shows the regression results using the same data as in Table 5.1, but this time we include combinations of time and country fixed effects as additional controls for factors that matter, as well as those control variables already included. As we can see in column one, when adding the time fixed effect to the regression (but excluding all other controls), the negative inequality effect on health remains. The negative correlation can therefore not be explained by the assumption that time has improved health and increased equality in all countries (which we hardly expected in the first place). Next, we account for variation among countries by introducing a dummy variable for each country, that is, a country fixed effect. It should be noted that the country fixed effect allows for all invariant observed and unobserved (or unobservable) factors that distinguish countries, and the inequality effect is therefore estimated by comparing what happens within countries when inequality changes. Column two shows that this drastically decreases the inequality effect, and it is no longer statistically

---

[18]   In our case, this results in a variable that is given the value of 1 for all observations made in the year 1970 and 0 for all other years. Another dummy variable is given the value 1 for observations made 1971–5 and so on until the last time period (2001–5). Another common way of using dummy variables in statistical analysis is to let the variable indicate people's gender and in this manner see if there is a systematic difference between men and women.

Table 5.3   *Correlation between inequality and life expectancy*
            (country and time fixed effects)

Dependent variable:
life expectancy at birth

	Time FE	Country FE	Time and country FE		
Gini (t − 1)	−0.409***	0.001	−0.019	−0.021	0.010
	[0.042]	[0.019]	[0.016]	[0.015]	[0.017]
GDP per				1.558**	0.539
capita				[0.629]	[0.679]
Physicians					1.774***
					[0.271]
Nutrition					4.702***
					[1.381]
Number of observations	575	575	575	575	575
Number of countries	126	126	126	126	126

Notes: Panel corrected standard errors in brackets
*** p < 0.01, ** p < 0.05, * p < 0.1

Source: Authors' analysis of the data provided by Bergh and Nilsson (2010).

significantly different from zero. This means that variables that influence both population health and inequality were most likely left out of the earlier analysis. Column three shows the estimation accounting for the fact that both income inequality and life expectancy have increased and that countries differ in ways that we cannot fully observe, although this does not change the result. The negative effect of the Gini coefficient on population health is not significantly different from zero and is therefore not statistically ensured.

Not all factors lose their significance in relation to population health when we include time and country fixed effects in the analysis. In column three, we see that adding GDP per capita seems to matter for health even when we are studying only changes over time within countries. The coefficient, however, decreases in both size and significance when we include physician density and caloric intake in column five. This means that GDP per capita does not improve health by itself but by allowing for higher physician density and higher caloric intake. GDP per capita is statistically significant in column four, which does not include physician density or caloric intake.

Summarizing the results so far, we note that the existence of a correlation between inequality and health across countries does not reflect what happens in a country when the level of inequality changes. A politician seeking guidance from the research on the determinants of population health should examine Table 5.2. If an increase in GDP per capita is used for spending in the health-care sector such that the density of physicians improves, then there is support for the view that this will improve average health over a five-year period. It should be noted, however, that the effects are generally smaller when estimated using country and time fixed effects compared with the results when these effects were not considered, as in Table 5.1.

5.4.3   Analysing Changes over Extended Time Periods

Studying changes over time is one method that is often used to avoid mistakes due to spurious correlations. If something irregular affects individual countries and greatly influences the level of average health or inequality, this country will play an important role when we plot the line that describes the correlation in levels (as in Figures 5.1 and 5.2). However, if this country's characteristics are roughly constant over time, which is arguably the case for many institutional variables, it is possible to use changes in inequality and changes in health outcomes to examine whether countries in which inequality has increased are also those that have become more unhealthy (or have obtained smaller improvements in their average health status).

Figure 5.6 illustrates what this analysis of changes might look like. Specifically, it shows the correlation between an increase in the level of inequality over the 1982–98 period and an increase in life expectancy over the 1986–2005 period (that is, a difference specification) for all countries for which we have access to data. We have, in other words, examined the change in inequality over the maximum amount of time permitted by our data, and we examine the extent to which these changes correlate systematically with changes in life expectancy. From the figure, it is clear to the naked eye that most countries experienced improvements in health (the exceptions are largely countries that have been particularly affected by HIV/AIDS). Apart from that, there is hardly any correlation to talk about. When

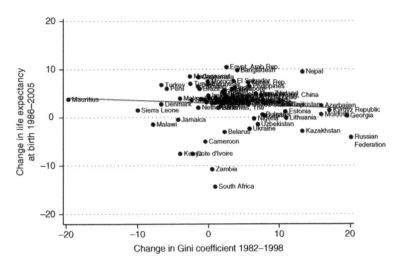

Source: Bergh and Nilsson (2010).

Figure 5.6   *Changes in inequality (1982–98) and life expectancy*
             (1986–2005) in rich and poor countries

a trend line is plotted using the least squares method, it becomes
clear that countries that have experienced increases in inequality
have experienced somewhat smaller increases in life expectancy.

One problem with the correlation in Figure 5.6 is that the considered time intervals overlap. If the effect of inequality on health can
be seen only after several years, the effect might not yet be visible
in available data. The ideal time lag between cause and effect is
typically unknown, which means that researchers must guess when
health outcomes should be measured.

However, there is another factor that we have not yet taken into
consideration: several scholars have argued that the inequality effect
is expected in rich countries but not necessarily in poor countries.[19]
Therefore, in Table 5.4, we show the regression results of difference
estimations, where the dependent variable is the difference in life
expectancy from 1990 to 2005, and the explanatory variable is the
difference in inequality during the 1982–90 period. The assumption

---

[19]   Deaton (2003), however, emphasizes that most of the explanations for why
inequality is a health risk are as reasonable for rich countries as for poor countries.

Table 5.4   Correlation between inequality and life expectancy

Dependent variable: change in life expectancy at birth 1990–2005

	All	All	All	Rich	Poor
Change Gini 1982–90	−0.026 [0.061]	0.010 [0.066]	−0.008 [0.065]	0.081 [0.199]	0.045 [0.082]
Life expectancy at birth 1990		0.105* [0.059]	0.228* [0.136]	0.543 [0.333]	0.105 [0.160]
GDP per capita			−1.209 [1.023]	−1.127 [1.547]	0.482 [2.044]
Number of countries	85	85	85	47	38

Notes: Robust standard errors in brackets
*** p < 0.01, ** p < 0.05, * p < 0.1

Source: Authors' own calculations based on the data presented in Bergh and Nilsson (2010).

here, in other words, is that relatively distant changes in inequality affect people's health.[20] As we can see in the table, there is no support for an inequality effect, even when we study only the pure correlation between changes in inequality and changes in health. A likely explanation for this result is that it is much more difficult to generate life expectancy improvements if life expectancy is already high, which was the case in many of the most equal countries by 1990. When examining life expectancy at the beginning of the period, however, we find that, if anything, the pattern occurs in the other direction: countries with high life expectancies at the beginning of the period also experienced the sharpest increases in life expectancy. This result, however, does not hold after we adjust for economic growth over the 1990–2005 period. As expected, there is a positive correlation between economic growth and improved population health.

Finally, Wilkinson (1986) argues that the inequality effect is only present in rich countries that have experienced the so-called epidemiological transition.[21] In columns four and five of Table 5.4, we

---

[20]   We have decided to refrain from making adjustments for caloric intake and physician density in order to make this test more on par with the inequality hypothesis, as these are considered mechanisms in the causal connection from inequality to health.

[21]   In countries that have experienced the epidemiological transition, most fatalities

examine whether there is any support for this notion by dividing the sample into rich and poor countries. The relevant threshold in this context, according to Wilkinson, is a GDP per capita of US $5,000 at 1990 prices.[22] However, we see that there does not seem to be an inequality effect in either rich or poor countries. The only variable that is statistically significant is life expectancy at birth in 1990 in the sample of rich countries – and, as before, the effect here is positive.

5.5   CONCLUSIONS

This chapter has presented a relatively technical and detailed description of how social scientists empirically analyse causal relationships. Our purpose was to show how results tend to change as various methodological difficulties arise and are considered.

To begin with, we have seen a fairly large negative correlation between income inequality and life expectancy in simple scatter plots. This correlation was reduced by one-half by accounting for differences in national income levels. However, as soon as we adjust for country-specific features that remain constant over time (as in country fixed effects), then there is no link whatsoever between the level of inequality and life expectancy. The same finding comes out from using a difference approach and examining whether the countries that experienced increases in inequality during the 1980s generally had slower increases in life expectancy during the 1990–2005 period. Increased inequality is not followed by a lower level of population health as measured in life expectancy. We summarize these results in Figure 5.7.

Accordingly, one conclusion from this chapter is that there is reason to question the sort of inferences we can draw from the existing literature on inequality and health. Many studies of the inequality effect on population health do not include many control variables

---

can be attributed to chronic illness rather than infectious diseases. Wilkinson (1996) argues that as countries grow richer and experience the epidemiological transition, major differences in mortality between countries shift from material scarcity (causing poverty and infectious diseases) to social disadvantages (causing stress and chronic diseases).

[22]   We distinguish between rich and poor countries based on the value of GDP per capita in 1982 using the 1996 price level. A rich country has a GDP per capita above US $5,000.

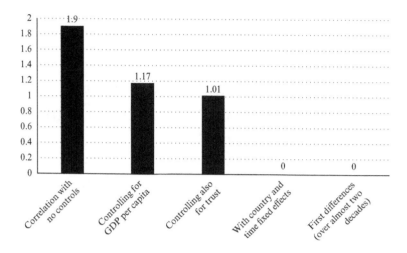

Figure 5.7   *Size of the inequality effect with different statistical*
specifications: number of years by which life expectancy
decreases when the Gini coefficient increased by 10 (on a
scale of 0–100)

besides GDP per capita and, as our simple analysis shows, this can
seriously affect the results if variables are omitted from the equation.
Furthermore, few studies use longitudinal data or account for time
and country fixed effects, despite the fact that most scholars today
agree that such effects exist and can make a difference (indeed, they
did in our empirical exercise). Once again, these inadequate methods
are important drivers of the conclusions we draw.

We hope that the reader carries with them these lessons on the
possibilities and hazards of using statistical analysis as we move on
to describe and interpret the findings in the existing literature on
income inequality and health.

6. The ecological fallacy: what conclusions can be drawn from group averages?

In the preceding chapter, we discussed various methods of statistical analysis that can be used to analyse the correlation between life expectancy and inequality. Our empirical examples showed correlations between variables in levels and changes, both with and without additional control variables. However, all the regressions had in common that they were based on aggregate data, with observations being population averages or sums. These regressions related inequality in a particular country to the average life expectancy in that same country. However, it is not necessarily the case that a correlation at the aggregate level implies a correlation at the individual level. Conclusions about individuals based on aggregate data are vulnerable to the so-called *ecological fallacy*. An ecological fallacy manifests when the correlations produced by aggregate observations are different from the correlations in the underlying individual observations (Robinson, 1950). To attribute a group trait to individuals within that group can thus be a mistake.[1]

In this chapter, we discuss the importance of moving from aggregate to individual data and how this shift influences the analysis of the inequality effect and (possibly) the results. We devote a chapter

---

[1] To illustrate the concept of ecological fallacy, Robinson (1950) used the correlation of being born abroad and being literate at the state level in the USA. These traits have a positive correlation at the state level, which would indicate that immigrants have higher levels of literacy than those born in the USA, whereas the correlation is negative at the individual level. The aggregate correlation resulted from immigrants – who are actually less literate than the native population – tending to settle in states whose native populations have generally higher levels of education. Robinson argued that all attempts to reach conclusions regarding individual behaviour or traits using aggregate data inevitably lead to ecological fallacies. Nevertheless, quite a few studies have been published on the possibility of making these kinds of conclusions by, for instance, focusing on the conditions that need to be fulfilled (Hammond, 1973; Langbein and Lichtman, 1978).

to this issue because hundreds of previous studies have used aggregate variables exclusively. In contrast, recent research has benefitted
from the creation of new individual-level databases, opening up the
possibility of examining whether a statistically significant correlation
between inequality and health at the aggregate (that is, country or
state) level reflects a similar correlation between individual health
and inequality at some level of society.

In an article published in 1998, British health economist
Hugh Gravelle emphasises that the risk of ecologic fallacy is due
to the tendency of relationship between an individual's income and
their level of health to be non-linear (Gravelle, 1998). The problem
noticed by Gravelle had already been detected by Rodgers (1979),
who showed that a negative effect of inequality on health could be
found even if inequality has no impact whatsoever on the health of
the individual.

Gravelle's hypothesis can be explained using simple graphs illus-
trating the correlation between income and health at the individual
level. The correlation is positive, which means that the higher your
income, the healthier you are. However, the relationship between
income and health is non-linear, and the positive correlation is
weakened as the level of income rises. Now, imagine a society that
consists of two individuals, Anna and Cecilia, and that their
monthly incomes are €2,000 and €6,000, respectively. Society's
average monthly income is €4,000 and Anna and Cecilia can be cat-
egorized as low- and high-income earners, respectively. If one were
to measure the average level of health in this society $\overline{H}$, it would be
the sum of Anna and Cecilia's levels of health divided by two. Figure
6.1 illustrates this situation.[2]

Now, assume that Anna's income decreases to €1,500 while
Cecilia's income remains the same, a situation shown in Figure 6.2.
Society's income dispersion increases because of this change, and
both average income $\overline{I}$ and average health $\overline{H}$ decline. At the individual level, Anna's health diminishes while Cecilia's health remains
the same because her income is unchanged. At the aggregate level,
therefore, there is a *negative* correlation between income inequality
and health.

Let us instead assume that Cecilia's income rises from €6,000 to

---

[2]   Note that we limit ourselves to a situation in which a person's health depends only
on her income.

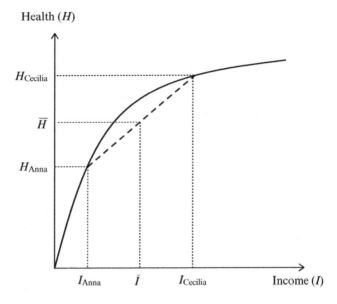

Figure 6.1   Baseline

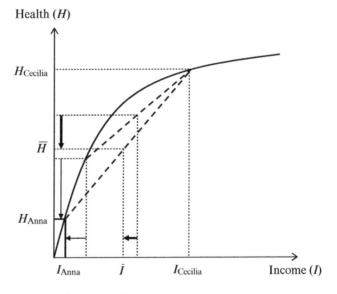

Figure 6.2   Low-income decrease

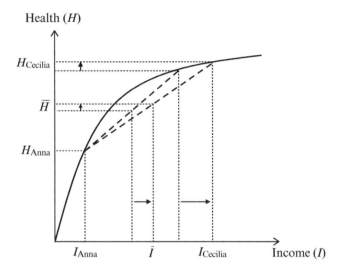

Figure 6.3   High-income increase

€6,500 while Anna's income remains the same at €2,000. This situation is shown in Figure 6.3. As we can see, the result is increased income dispersion, while the average health level is improved because Cecilia's health improves and Anna's health (and income) remains the same. In other words, there is now a *positive* correlation between income inequality and population health.

Finally, let us assume that both Anna and Cecilia's incomes simultaneously change as described in the examples above: Anna's income decreases by €500 and Cecilia's increases by €500. This situation is shown in Figure 6.4. The change widens the distribution of income even more than the previous cases, but it does not change average income. What then happens to population health? Cecilia's health will improve while Anna's health will worsen. As a result of the nonlinear relationship between individual health and income, Anna's health will worsen by more than Cecilia's will improve. This means that the average level of health is lower after the increase in the dispersion of the income distribution. Once again, we find a *negative* correlation between inequality and health.

When we compare the income distributions and average health of different societies, we can assume that we will find a correlation

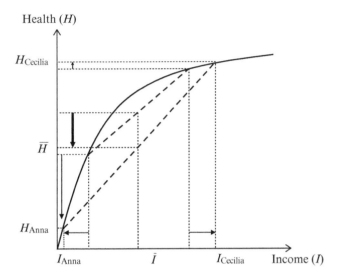

Figure 6.4   Low-income decrease and high-income increase

between differences in income and poor health for the simple reason that increasing income is less beneficial to the health of the rich than to that of the poor. A policy that redistributes income from the rich to the poor can, for the same reason, be expected to increase population health. The same is true for a policy that increases everyone's income by the same amount.

What happens if everyone's income increases but the incomes of the rich increase at a greater rate than that of the poor? To answer this question, we need to go beyond the illustration in the above figures and determine whether the health of individuals is a function of the income distribution at some level of the society in which they live, apart from their own incomes.

A correlation at the aggregate level between inequality and health is consistent with the theory that inequality is detrimental to people's health, but it does prove this to be the case: the same correlation would result if the only thing that matters for an individual's health is their own income. In addition, Wagstaff and van Doorslaer (2000) notice that the same correlation is consistent with the theory that a person's health depends on their income in relation to the average income in society (or any other reference group).[3] This means that there are at least three explanations for why a correlation between inequality and population health exists at the country level. These three explanations have been formulated as well-known hypotheses in this field of research:

- the absolute income hypothesis;
- the relative income hypothesis;
- the income inequality hypothesis.

According to the *absolute income hypothesis* (AIH), what matters to health is the level of individuals' own material resources independently of the material resources of others. In our example above, the *level effect* means that Cecilia is healthier than Anna. Furthermore, the AIH stipulates that the marginal increase in health as income increases is decreasing (as in Figure 6.1), that is, an increase in income for each individual makes everyone more healthy, although the health gain Anna receives is greater than the gain Cecilia receives.

The *relative income hypothesis* (RIH) says that what matters for the health of the individual is how their income relates to the incomes of others in society (either in relation to the whole population or to some sub-group within society). According to this hypothesis, there is a *comparison effect* on health such that individuals who note that others' incomes increase while their own remains the same will experience a decrease in health.

Finally, according to the *income inequality hypothesis* (IIH), the dispersion of the income distribution in society has an independent effect on individual health. The *inequality effect* suggests that inequality as such negatively affects health. According to the IIH, an individual whose income remains the same in a society with an average income that also remains the same will experience worsening health as income inequality increases. In the example in Figure 6.2, where income inequality increased due to Anna's falling income, the

---

[3]   Wagstaff and van Doorslaer (2000) also show that that the correlation between economic inequality and public health corresponds with a situation in which an individual's health is determined by their rank on the income distribution or their relative level of deprivation. As this kind of correlation has been given scant attention in the literature, we chose not to provide a detailed account of these hypotheses. For a comprehensive account, see Wagstaff and van Doorslaer (2000).

IIH suggests that Cecilia will experience worse health even though Anna's income has changed.

6.1   HOW CAN THE THREE EFFECTS BE DIFFERENTIATED?

With access to individual information about income and health, it is possible to separate the three effects from each other. We do this by continuing the example above, extending the analysis to a third person, Bernard, whose income is between that of Anna and Cecilia. Table 6.1 shows various scenarios in which Anna, Bernard and Cecilia earn different incomes. Note that Bernard's income is the same in all cases, and we wish to see what the hypotheses stipulate about his health.

The first column in Table 6.1 shows the original income distribution. Compared to this distribution, scenario 1 shows a situation wherein Anna's income is €500 lower and Cecilia's is €500 higher. The average income of the group remains the same in scenario 1 as in the baseline, whereas the level of economic inequality increases from 0.22 to 0.28 as measured by the Gini coefficient. According to the IIH, Bernard's health will be lower in scenario 1 compared to the original distribution. According to the RIH, Bernard will be healthier in scenario 3: his income of $4,000 is $300 above the average income compared with scenario 2, where his income is $200 below the average (please note that scenarios 2 and 3 have been set up so that the Gini coefficient remains the same). If neither income inequality nor relative income matters, then Bernard will have the

Table 6.1   Four monthly income scenarios for Anna, Bernard and Cecilia (€)

	Original distribution	Scenario 1	Scenario 2	Scenario 3
Anna	2,000	1,500	2,500	2,000
Bernard	4,000	4,000	4,000	4,000
Cecilia	6,000	6,500	6,000	5,100
Average	4,000	4,000	4,200	3,700
Gini	0.22	0.28	0.19	0.19

same level of health in all four cases, whereas Anna and Cecilia's health will vary with their incomes according to the AIH.

Note that in this example, we have no information about the individuals' absolute health levels and are therefore unable to distinguish among the three hypotheses. However, the example clearly demonstrates that we need individual data to understand an observed correlation between inequality and health at the aggregate level. The three explanations are in fact fully compatible: the level effect, the comparison effect and the inequality effect could very well coexist. If, for instance, both the level effect and the inequality effect exist, it is not clear what happens to population health if everyone gets richer while inequality increases. Absolute income improves population health, while the inequality effect works in the opposite direction. The overall effect is therefore dependent on which, if any, of these effects is most influential.

6.2   THE DIFFICULTY OF CHOOSING A REFERENCE GROUP

It follows from the line of reasoning presented above that both the relative income hypothesis and the inequality hypothesis imply that an individual's well-being is influenced by relative economic conditions. This says nothing, however, about which reference group should be seen as the most relevant when examining this issue. The society we described in the above hypothetical examples could be a workplace, a neighbourhood, city, region, country or any other group to which people compare themselves.

On the theme of reference groups, consider the common English expression *keeping up with the Joneses*. This idiom was coined in the USA during the 1950s and reflected a typical middle-class family in the US suburbs; it, captures people's tendencies to compare themselves to their neighbours and to value their own situation in relation to the material well-being of their neighbours. The RIH can therefore be evaluated by examining whether the average income in a geographical area has an effect on individual health besides what can be explained by individual income alone. This hypothesis has been analysed often in recent research. There is, however, nothing that suggests that people necessarily compare themselves to others who are geographically nearby. Nor is it obvious that – as in the

example of Anna, Bernard and Cecilia – everyone compares themselves to everyone. As discussed by Nobel laureate Angus Deaton
(2003) and Miller and Paxson (2006), it may prove difficult to test the
RIH because the reference group can be created using a number of
different criteria. For example, people might compare themselves to
others with a similar education, age or job. What constitutes a relevant reference group probably also depends on the context in which
people live (for example, if you are studying rich or poor countries;
see, for instance, Karlsson et al., 2010).

A number of sociological studies note that reference groups tend
to be limited to relatively similar people, for instance, family, friends,
neighbours and colleagues (Frank, 1985; Merton, 1957). Runciman
(1966) suggests that people may compare themselves to individuals who they want to emulate or surpass. There is also a growing
literature in economics that examines the composition of reference
groups. Knight, Song and Gunatilaka (2009), Senik (2009) and
Clark and Senik (2010) represent a few interesting contributions that
make use of data from lifestyle surveys to determine who individuals
primarily compare themselves to. This literature confirms the asser-
tion that we mainly compare ourselves to people in our proximity.
Using Chinese household data, Knight, Song and Gunatilaka establish that 60 per cent of respondents compare themselves to individuals in their own villages (that is, to people where they live and work).
Using data from 30 European countries, Clark and Senik conclude
that the most common reference group is work colleagues. Senik
reaches the same conclusion in her investigation of this question in
Central and Eastern Europe, but she also finds that people often
compare themselves to their former classmates.

The inequality effect is usually tested by analysing whether income
inequality within a certain region influences individual health. The
choice of region should, ideally, reflect the mechanisms expected
to play a part. On the one hand, if we believe that factors such as
trust and social cohesion explain the correlation between inequality
and health, then it is relevant for us to examine whether inequality, measured at a relatively local geographical level, influences the
individuals' well-being. If, on the other hand, we believe that the
most significant mechanism is public policy, then we should measure
economic inequality in the regions that are relevant to politics (for
example, cities or counties). According to Wilkinson (1997), what
matters most to people's health is the inequality present in relatively

large geographical areas, such as federal states or whole countries.[4] This means that a thorough test of the inequality hypothesis would require individual data on health and income, in addition to data on income inequality for a number of countries or large regions. For this reason, Wilkinson's hypothesis requires a massive amount of data to test and is complicated to evaluate.[5]

---

[4] Although Wilkinson argues that the inequality effect is a result of people making social comparisons, he believes that inequality measured in the direct vicinity of one's home (as in neighbourhood) does not reflect the inequality effect, as people living close to one another tend to be relatively similar (homogenous).

[5] Note that of the large number of studies referred to in *The Spirit Level* (Wilkinson and Pickett, 2009), only a handful contain data that is sufficiently detailed to distinguish among the absolute income, relative income and income inequality effects.

7. Income inequality and health: what does the literature tell us?

This chapter provides an extensive review of the research on the inequality effect on health. To emphasize the importance of using individual-level data to understand the association between inequality and health, we limit ourselves to studies that use individual- or household-level data. The survey is focused on the income inequality effect, which (apart from the absolute income effect) is the hypothesis that has been tested most frequently in the literature. We are thus interested in studies that examine the effect of population inequality on individual health.[1]

A large number of previous studies have analysed the link between income inequality and population health. One of the first studies testing the inequality hypothesis in this manner found that income inequality was associated with both infant mortality and life expectancy at age five, using data for 56 developed and developing countries (Rodgers, 1979). A clear majority of the following studies using population data has also found support for the inequality hypothesis, many of the studies focusing on objective health measures, such as Pampel and Pillai (1986), child mortality; Duleep (1995), adult mortality; Pickett et al., (2005), obesity. A recent review also states that several recently published articles using aggregate variables provide substantial new evidence that equality will improve population health and well-being (Pickett and Wilkinson, 2015).

However, we saw in Chapter 6 that investigations that do not use individual data risk falling prey to the ecological fallacy, which means that aggregate-level analyses cannot differentiate among absolute income-level effects, relative income effects and inequality effects on

---

[1] It is worth stressing that this is different from, for example, Link and Phelan's (1995) theory of social conditions as fundamental causes of health inequalities, according to which socioeconomic status affects health via income, knowledge, prestige, power and social connectedness.

health.[2] Even though the ecological fallacy argument, originally proposed by Gravelle (1998), is now uncontroversial, there is some disagreement in the literature about how the extent to which the ecological fallacy affects the results. While Gravelle's study described the correlation between population health and income inequality as merely an artefact, Babones (2008) argues that correcting for individual income only accounts for a small part of the correlation between inequality and population health across countries. Our literature review suggests that all studies that are able to compare aggregate effects with and without individual controls find that the inequality effect on health becomes weaker. In some cases, it decreases but remains significant (see, e.g., Karlsson et al., 2010; Chang and Christakis, 2005; Meara, 1999), while in others, it disappears altogether (see e.g., Fiscella and Franks, 1997; Gerdtham and Johannesson, 2004).

Regardless of whether the effect of controlling for individual income is large or small, it is still the case that studies using individual-level data offer more reliable evidence of the magnitude of an observed inequality effect. Magnitudes are, as discussed in Chapter 4, important when assessing the effects of redistributive policies on health compared with other policies that are aimed at improving the level of health.

However, the reader should recall that the use of individual data is not an Alexander cut to solve the problem of causality. We tried to show in Chapter 5 that the link between inequality and individual health might be dual: a person's health can be affected by or itself affect income. In addition, we saw that the problems caused by omitted variables in the empirical analysis of inequality and health do not disappear merely because individual data are used. Mellor and Milyo (2002) argue that scholars should include country/region and time fixed effects when using individual-level data.

We would also like to reiterate the argument made by Leigh et al. (2009) that the direction of causality is only relevant if and when there is a clear correlation. Studies that do not find a correlation between income inequality and individual health thus refute the notion that inequality causes bad health, as well as the notion that bad health causes inequality.

---

[2]   For this reason, we do not discuss relevant contributions to the debate on the effect of income inequality on health that rely on empirical analyses of aggregate data (for example, Kaplan et al., 1996; Lynch et al., 2000; Mackenbach, 2002).

To ascertain the level of quality of the reviewed findings, we limit our survey to studies published in peer-reviewed scientific journals, that is, articles that have been scrutinized by other academics in order to validate the research and its results.[3] In addition to these two criteria – peer-reviewed articles using micro-level data to analyse the inequality effect – we only cover articles published in English.

One unique feature of our survey is that we acknowledge that this literature is essentially interdisciplinary. For this reason, we searched bibliographic databases for articles in psychiatry, psychology, sociology, epidemiology, medicine and economics that met the requirements stated above. We followed-up with a 'snowball search' focusing on citations from the five most recent studies of the IIH. Arguably, this makes our survey one of the most comprehensive to date in terms of disciplinary breadth.

As several of the studies mentioned are discussed only briefly, we have compiled all the studies included in this survey in a summary table in the Appendix. The table presents the main results of all studies and provides detailed information, such as the hypotheses being tested, which reference groups and countries are considered, and the data used.

The chapter begins by discussing the results of studies examining the correlation between economic inequality and individual health at the sub-national level (for example, states or counties in the USA, Bundesländer in Germany, or municipalities in Sweden). Thereafter, we account for studies examining the relationship between income inequality and individual health in several countries at the same time. If inequality at the national level is what truly matters for health outcomes, these studies are the most relevant.

Finally, we devote a special section to studies of the *relative income effect* on individual health. As explained above, here we assume that what matters to good health is the individual's relative income in relation to that of others rather than the absolute level of income – the *absolute income effect* – or the degree of income inequality manifest in society – the *inequality effect*. The number of scientific papers testing the RIH has, until recently, been quite small but has increased in recent years.

---

[3]   Peer review has been a formal part of scientific communication for more than three centuries, and reviewers are central to scholarly publishing.

7.1 THE INEQUALITY EFFECT IN SINGLE COUNTRIES: OBJECTIVE HEALTH OUTCOMES

There has been a sharp increase in the number of studies empirically analysing how inequality in a single country affects the health of its citizens. Most of these studies focus on industrialized, rich countries, and the majority looks at the USA. The focus on rich countries, largely disregarding the experiences of less developed countries, is partly the result of Wilkinson's hypothesis that income inequality is only detrimental to health once a society reaches a certain level of material wealth.[4]

In this section, we first examine single-country studies based on objective health measures, and in the next section consider studies based on subjective health measures.

Mortality is one of the most common objective health measures in the literature. Using mortality outcomes in nationally representative data for the USA, neither Daly et al. (1998) nor Mellor and Milyo (2003) find any significant negative association with income inequality in US states during the late 1980s or the 1990s. Fiscella and Franks (1997), studying the inequality effect using data on inequality within US communities, arrive at the same conclusion. They first observe that there is a considerable negative and significant correlation between income inequality and mortality but then conclude that the correlation disappears when the income of each household is included in the analysis. In line with the argument presented by Gravelle (1998) on the aggregation problem (the ecological fallacy), poverty rather than income inequality seems to be associated with poor health. Likewise, Blakely et al. (2003) conclude that there is no significant association between regional inequality in the USA and adult mortality after adjusting for household income and ethnicity in the regressions.

The situation in Sweden has been thoroughly investigated by Gerdtham and Johannesson (2004). The authors use a random selection of more than 40,000 individuals living in various parts of the country. These individuals were interviewed in the mid-1980s and then followed-up regarding mortality 10–17 years later. The

---

[4] Naturally, the availability of adequate data is generally much better for relatively rich countries.

relationship between income inequality and mortality is tested using a number of measures for the income distribution, which are calculated based on municipalities and counties. The income data used in the study is from public tax authority records.

In the first step of their analysis, Gerdtham and Johannesson take the characteristics of each individual into account – characteristics such as income and previous health status as stated in the first interview. There is no indication that income inequality is linked to higher mortality in Sweden. In the second step of the analysis, the sensitivity of the results is tested in regressions that do not consider individual characteristics. Not even in this less restrictive context is there evidence of an inequality effect.

Studies of other Nordic countries examining the relationship between inequality and objective health have found somewhat conflicting results. Osler et al. (2002) use data on mortality from 25,000 inhabitants of the Greater Copenhagen region in Denmark – who were tracked over the 1976–94 period – and conclude that there is no significant correlation with inequality at the national level. The same conclusion is reached by Martikainen et al. (2004), who investigate whether inequality increases the risk of suicide in Finland. On the one hand, these results, and the lack of an inequality effect in Sweden discussed above, may indicate that the negative effect on health is insignificant in comparatively equal societies with extensive welfare states. On the other hand, Dahl et al. (2006) find evidence of a positive correlation between regional income inequality and mortality in Norway. Using a cross-sectional analysis of individual data on all men and women aged 26–66 in the country (over 2 million individuals), the authors observe a significant effect of inequality on individual health during the 1990s.

Studies using other objective health measures also tend to find only weak links between income inequality and objective health. Meara (1999) takes advantage of the great deal of available information on children and their mothers in the USA to analyse the relationship between income inequality and children's health. When household and individual characteristics are taken into account in the empirical analysis, there is no significant correlation between child health and inequality across US states, regardless of whether the analysis focuses on birth weight or child mortality.

Shifting focus to hospitalization and diagnoses of acute disease with prominent symptoms and with a high likelihood of hospitalization,

Henriksson et al. (2010) explore the relationship between income inequality and individual incidents of acute myocardial infarction (heart attack) across Swedish municipalities. If anything, the risk for heart attack was lower in areas with higher income inequality. Also using data for Sweden, Grönqvist et al. (2012) investigate the IIH in a natural experiment. They make use of a settlement policy in which authorities assigned refugees an area of residence and focus on longitudinal administrative hospitalization records. This is one of few studies that really trues to tackle potential endogeneity problems. The findings suggest no statistically significant effects of income inequality on objective health.

Overweight and obesity are two other objective health outcomes that have been used in this literature. Looking at recent evidence in the USA, Chang and Christakis (2005) do not find any evidence of an inequality effect in their analysis of the relationship between obesity, as measured by a BMI, and the income distribution in larger cities. A more recent study even suggests that higher county-level (but not state-level) inequality in the USA is associated with a lower likelihood of being obese (Chen and Crawford, 2012). In contrast to the clear majority of studies on inequality and objective health within the USA, Zheng and George (2012) find support for the inequality hypothesis (particularly for men) in their analysis of individuals' physical functioning measured as variables capturing whether an individual needed help with personal care, routine needs and activity limitations. Inequality is measured by the Gini coefficient and various income decile ratios and calculated on a national level over the 1984–2007 period.

Mental health is yet another objective health measure that has been used in the literature. Bechtel et al. (2012) test the IIH in an Australian context focusing on the mental component of the SF-36 measure (see Ware et al., 2000), which corresponds to a rich set of items covering feeling nervous, peaceful, sad or happy that are transformed into a score. Using a variety of inequality indices, they find no evidence of an inequality effect.

While Wilkinson and Pickett (1996) suggest that the inequality effect of health should only appear in rich countries, Deaton (2003) claims that the mechanisms noted as explanations of the IIH in rich countries are also plausible in poor countries. Setting aside high-income countries and focusing on analyses of objective health using data from middle- and low-income countries, four studies support the IIH to some extent. Chiavegatto Filho et al. (2013) explore the associations among income inequality, depression, mental disorders and anxiety in São Paolo, Brazil. The results suggest that individuals living in metropolitan areas with high inequality are more likely to suffer from depression, while no similar results were found with respect to the other health outcomes analysed. Subramanian et al. (2007) find that income inequality at the federal state level in India is correlated with a higher risk of being both over- as well as underweight among women. Similar conclusions can be arrived at from the results provided by Chen and Meltzer (2008). They find a correlation between income inequality and being overweight, as well as having high blood pressure, when studying inhabitants of rural areas in China over a period of nine years. However, Nilsson and Bergh (2014) find that higher income inequality is associated with better child health in Zambia. Using individual-level data on nutritional health, the results suggest a positive relationship across various geographical aggregations – that is, when inequality is measured at the regional, district and constituency levels.[5]

Altogether, the empirical evidence for an income inequality effect is weak when using objective health measurements – particularly in rich countries such as the USA, the UK, Sweden, Denmark, Australia and New Zealand. Evidence in favour of the inequality effect is, however, found for Norway and middle-income countries such as Brazil, India and China.

7.2   THE INEQUALITY EFFECT IN SINGLE COUNTRIES: SUBJECTIVE HEALTH OUTCOMES

Contrary to the weak evidence of an inequality effect for objective health measurements, the results from studies of single countries using subjective health measurements indicate that there is in fact a significant association between inequality and lower subjective health.

---

[5]   The positive relationship could be explained by the relationship between inequality and purchasing power, or by food sharing in low-income countries, in turn generating a more equal consumption distribution than the observed income distribution (Nilsson and Bergh, 2014).

As already noted, many studies focus on experiences in the USA. For example, Lillard et al. (2015) and Zheng (2009) examine the IIH using national data on inequality in the USA over several decades. Both articles find a significant negative association with self-reported health.

Looking at a cross-state individual data set in the USA, Shi and Starfield (2000) show that inequality at the federal-state level negatively influences self-reported health, even when individual characteristics such as income, age and risk behaviour are taken into consideration. Kennedy et al. (1998) conclude that the probability of reporting poor health is as much as 30 per cent higher for individuals living in US states, with the highest levels of variation in the income distribution compared with those living in the most equal states. Similarly, LeClere and Soobader (2000), Fiscella and Franks (2000), Blakely et al. (2000) and Subramanian and Kawachi (2006) all find a negative health impact for individuals stemming from state-level inequality in the USA. It should be noted that many of these results are limited to certain groups in society. For example, the negative correlation noted by LeClere and Soobader (2000) is only present among young, white individuals, whereas income inequality does not seem to influence the health of African Americans or the elderly.

The magnitude and significance of the correlation between inequality and subjective health is considerably smaller and weaker, or even non-existent, in geographical areas smaller than the federal state. Blakely et al. (2002) fail to find evidence of an inequality effect on subjective health in major US metropolitan areas. This notion is confirmed by the results presented by Sturm and Gresenz (2002), who also use variation in income inequality across major metropolitan areas in the USA to identify the inequality effect. These scholars use both self-reported information from adults on the presence of various chronic medical problems and information on depression and anxiety. Regardless the choice of health measure, they do not find any results supporting the IIH. The role of the geographical level of analysis is also highlighted in a study by Chen and Crawford (2012), which takes a specific perspective on geographical aggregation. With respect to self-assessed health, their results suggest that individuals residing in US counties with high inequality report better health than their peers residing in more equal counties.

Turning to the situation in other countries, some studies examine the UK, which has become one of the most unequal European countries in recent years. Weich et al. (2001, 2002) conduct two cross-sectional studies focusing on various self-reported health measures. They find no statistical evidence that individual mental health is influenced by the distribution of income, but they do find a significant negative correlation between inequality and self-reported health for some inequality measurements. In an extensive investigation, Gravelle and Sutton (2009) analyse the presence of a British inequality effect using a different type of data: a recurring cross-section for the 1979–2000 period, where the information on regional inequality is measured repeatedly but where individuals are observed only once. Their analysis illustrates the importance of paying attention to time trends in statistical analyses. The initial results show a negative correlation between inequality and self-reported health, as do the results in Weich et al. (2002). The initial inequality effect, however, turns out to be a spurious correlation because inequality captures time trends in income inequality and health outcomes. When time variables are considered, there is actually a significant, positive correlation between increased inequality and improved subjective health. This conclusion is also supported by Craig (2005) who, in his study of Scotland, shows that the self-reported health is better for individuals living in municipalities that are more unequal.

Other countries have also been studied. For example, Shibuya et al. (2002) and Aida et al. (2011) find a strong negative correlation between regional income inequality in Japan and self-reported health. This association, however, vanishes when the income of the respondents and their socio-demographic characteristics – such as age, gender or marital status – are included in the analysis. Similar results are found in analyses of the IIH and subjective health in Hong Kong (Wong et al., 2009), Canada (McLeod et al., 2003) and Spain (Karlsdotter et al., 2012). A recent study of the urban capital area of Stockholm, however, finds a moderate, negative and significant association between inequality and self-rated poor health at the municipality level, but the relationship disappears when reducing the aggregation level and examining neighbourhoods (Rostila et al., 2012).

Another approach is to focus on sub-groups of the population. Two recent studies look specifically at how income inequality influences the health of the elderly. Ichida et al. (2009) explore the relationship between subjective health and inequality among older people aged 65+ in Japan. The researchers find that individuals living in areas with high income inequality display poorer self-assessed health. Similarly, Feng et al. (2012) find support for the inequality hypothesis when analysing the effects of province inequality on self-rated health among individuals aged 80–112 and when controlling for individual and household characteristics. These studies are particularly interesting contributions if we believe that elderly people are more susceptible to societal inequality, as they are more dependent on others, and more vulnerable, as they are more reliant on the resources (such as health care) that are available where they reside.

Happiness and inequality, as well as their association within specific countries, have been examined by a smaller strand of the literature. As we discussed in Chapter 2, individual health is usually regarded as an important determinant of happiness. Empirical studies of what constitutes happiness therefore usually include health as an explanatory variable. This procedure, however, somewhat impedes the interpretation of the income inequality effect because in these cases individual health is a possible mechanism through which inequality may have an impact. Existing studies on happiness essentially confirm the results of other studies of subjective health outcomes. By using repeated cross-sectional data for individuals in the USA, Alesina et al. (2004) conclude that people living in states with higher levels of inequality tend to declare themselves as less happy, even when individual characteristics and time trends are taken into consideration in the empirical analysis. Similarly, Oishi et al. (2011) conclude that Americans seem to be happier in years with lower national income inequality. Their analysis makes use of longitudinal data over a 37-year period. Looking at studies for other countries than the USA offers a different perspective. Tomes (1986) is an early study conducted in the Canadian context, which finds no negative correlation between income inequality, as measured by the proportion of total incomes earned by the poorest 40 per cent in Canada's election districts, and individual happiness. The results of a separate analysis restricted to gender suggest that, if anything, income inequality is positively associated with the happiness of men. A positive correlation between income inequality and individual happiness is also observed by Clark (2003) in a study that makes use of data from the UK,[6] whereas Senik (2004) concludes that there is

---

[6] Clark (2003) uses information on income inequality within various reference groups, such as age and gender, rather than using geographically aggregated inequality measures.

no regional inequality effect on happiness when using cross-sectional data for Russia. A recent study on China further suggests that the relationship between inequality and happiness is more complex, exhibiting an inverted U shape, in line with Hirchman's tunnel effect (Wang et al., 2015).

How can one account for the fact that the negative correlation between income inequality and subjective health (including happiness) found in some countries such as the USA (even in studies correcting for individual characteristics) is partly related to the geographical area used when measuring inequality?[7] That is, there is a clear association when the income distribution is studied at the federal-state level or at the national level, but studies focusing on smaller geographical areas generally reject the IIH or arrive at the opposite conclusion. One possibility is that some variable(s) is (are) incorrectly left out of the equation. In other words, that one or several variables that are not taken into account in the examination explain why some states are more unequal and have worse health (and lower happiness). Identifying this or these variable(s) could prove difficult, but one could, for instance, argue that the level of corruption and other measures mirroring institutional quality in a society (generally referred to as formal and informal institutions) may influence both individual health and income inequality.

One way of approaching this issue is to see whether the inequality effect holds over longer periods. A longitudinal approach makes it possible for scholars to isolate the effects from regional or local differences that originate from formal and informal institutions and that are generally difficult to measure. A few studies begin from this methodological starting point. Mellor and Milyo (2002, 2003), for example, conclude that US state income inequality is associated with self-reported health when the economic and demographic characteristics are kept constant in the analysis. When differences across states are taken into consideration, however, the correlation disappears.[8] Likewise, Luttmer (2005) observes that there does not seem to be a

---

[7] This correlation does not exist in the USA alone. Oshio and Kobayashi (2010), for instance, find a similar effect in Japan. However, as with other studies, this study does not use data in a statistically optimal manner. Even though the authors have access to detailed information on household income, they chose to divide household incomes into three broad income categories. It is therefore reasonable to assume that household income actually explains more than the analysis in this study is able to capture.
[8] To reduce the risk that the correlation between income inequality and individual

significant correlation between income inequality in US neighbour-hoods and individual happiness when using longitudinal data.[9] Lorgelly and Lindley (2008) also follow a large sample of individu-als over a long period – this time in the UK – and are thus able to consider factors that may cause errors in cross-sectional studies. The association between inequality and self-reported health is tested using a number of different measures of the dispersion of the income distribution. This is done to consider the possibility that health effects can manifest differently depending on the kind of income distribution that is present in a society. The results of this longitudi-nal study, however, do not indicate that economic inequality has a detrimental effect on the health of the British people. Schwarze and Härpfer (2007), however, find evidence of an inequality effect on self-reported happiness in their panel study of German individuals who were followed over a 14-year period. These longitudinal studies find that the inequality effect at least partially reflects the effect on health compared with factors that differ across geographical regions and that we know to be important to people's health (such as differences in lifestyle). It is not possible to determine whether these factors are caused by income inequality or by something else.

Summing up, several single-country studies detect a negative inequality effect on subjective health. The effect seems to weaken when individual characteristics are accounted for, but in most cases it does not vanish entirely. This evidence thus stands in contrast to the findings of most studies using objective health measurements.

7.3 IS THERE A DELAYED INEQUALITY EFFECT ON HEALTH?

Most of the studies discussed so far consider instant correlation outcomes, assessing inequality and health at approximately the same point in time. However, if the health consequences of income inequality do not manifest until after a certain amount of time, it

---

health is the result of unobserved factors, Mellor and Milyo (2002, 2003) include dummy variables for all electoral areas in the statistical analysis.
[9] Luttmer (2005) measures inequality within US PUMAs, which are statistical geo-graphical areas defined for the dissemination of micro data with more than 100,000 inhabitants.

follows that at least some of the results of these studies need to be questioned. Wilkinson and Pickett (2010), for instance, argue that income inequality causes psychosocial stress, which leads to cardiovascular diseases and other stress-related diseases over time. The notion that inequality may affect political outcomes, such that health outcomes are eventually affected, implies that there could be a significant time lag before the effects of inequality are noticed in health measures. This might explain why the IIH is mostly confirmed by subjective health measurements. It is, in other words, possible that physical health, as measured by objective health measures, is only affected over the long term.

There are only a handful of studies so far that explore the existence of this delayed inequality effect; that is, if people's health is affected by previous income inequalities within the societies in which they reside. These studies yield mixed conclusions. Zheng (2012) investigates the long-term relationship between national-level income dispersion and mortality risk in the USA. By controlling for a series of preceding inequalities, the author finds that while there is no instantaneous relationship, income inequality has a negative impact on individual mortality risk with a time delay of five to 12 years. Also focusing on the role of national-level inequality but assessing its relationship to self-assessed health, the results of Lillard et al. (2015) suggest that income inequality experienced as a child matters for adult health. Focusing on a lower aggregation level, Blakely et al. (2000) claim that income inequality in US states lagged by 15 years is most strongly correlated with self-reported health. The effect of inequality 15 years ago, however, is not significantly different from the effect of present income inequality. Subramanian and Kawachi (2006), who study time delays of up to 25 years, and Karlsson et al. (2010), who study a time delay of ten years, conclude that the correlation between income inequality and self-reported health is essentially the same regardless of whether contemporary or historical inequality measures are used.

Some studies fail to find support for the inequality hypothesis using lagged measures. Gravelle and Sutton (2009), for example, do not find any detrimental effects of present regional inequality or of regional inequality lagged by one to five years on the self-reported health of British participants. Similar results are presented by Mellor and Milyo (2003) for the US context. Mellor and Milyo (2003) study the associations between different kinds of mortality (cardiovascular disease, cancer, murder and accidents) and the income distribution at the US state level lagged by 5–29 years. The researchers find only one statistically significant correlation: US states with a higher level of inequality have significantly lower mortality from cardiovascular diseases. This conflicts with the theory that inequality causes social stress, which in turn leads to more people dying from cardiovascular diseases. Overall, there is no clear evidence of a delayed inequality effect on people's health, and it is rare that studies find correlations between income inequality within countries and objective health measures at the individual level, even when using inequality data from as far back as 30 years.

7.4 IS EVERYONE AFFECTED EQUALLY BY THE INEQUALITY EFFECT?

Although the IIH asserts that everyone is affected the same way by increased income dispersion, it is not unreasonable to think that an increase in inequality might primarily influence the health of the worst off in society. In fact, quite a few scholars have tested this hypothesis by analysing the correlation across income groups. This hypothesis is sometimes referred to as the *weak income inequality hypothesis.* Methodologically, the assumption that inequality has a larger effect on some income brackets than on others is usually tested using an interaction variable. Apart from the descriptive value of such an investigation, this type of analysis provides clues about which mechanisms actually mediate the relationship between income inequality and poor health. For example, Gustavsson and Jordahl (2008) find that the correlation between economic inequality and interpersonal trust varies greatly across different groups in society. In particular, a strong correlation is observed between inequality and trust in groups with low incomes.

The empirical results are again somewhat mixed. On the one hand, Kahn et al. (2000), in a study on the mental health of US mothers, and Dahl et al. (2006), in a study focusing on individual determinants of mortality in Norway, conclude that income inequality primarily is a health risk for the poorest. Similar results are found in a separate analysis by Kennedy et al. (1998), who note that the general correlation between inequality and poor health across US states seems to be driven entirely by a negative impact on the well-being of poor individuals. These results suggest that an inequality effect on health exists but does not affect everyone within society, mainly influencing households and individuals with relatively limited economic resources. The same result can be seen in Schwarze and Härpfer (2007), where the inequality effect on happiness does not exist for those with medium to high incomes.

Several other studies find entirely different patterns. Wong et al. (2009) and Gerdtham and Johannesson (2004) do not find any evidence of an inequality effect on health outcomes – neither in the population nor among individuals of relatively low socioeconomic status. Similarly, Grönqvist et al. (2012) do not find that inequality is detrimental to health among a socioeconomically disadvantaged group of refugees in their analysis of the risk of being hospitalized. Weich et al. (2001) examine potential determinants of mental illness and find evidence that inequality is detrimental to health. Furthermore, this detrimental effect tends to increase rather than decrease with higher incomes. A similar picture emerges in a study of the association between economic inequality and happiness in the USA by Alesina et al. (2004). Based on regressions in which income inequality is interacted with income, these scholars conclude that the significant inequality effect occurs when the rich, rather than the poor, become unhappy due to large differences in income. Mellor and Milyo (2002), however, observe an overall positive effect on the health of the most economically needy individuals – considering individual specific characteristics – caused by inequality.

Thus, it seems as if some empirical studies show that an increase in income inequality, if anything, improves the health and well-being of the poorest segment of the population. Mellor and Milyo (2002) do not discuss possible mechanisms behind this inverse inequality effect on health, but the interpretation offered by Alesina et al. (2004) is in line with Hirschman's (1973) tunnel effect hypothesis (discussed in Chapter 4). This hypothesis states that poor Americans are not negatively affected by inequality, as they generally believe that they have good chances for upward social and financial mobility. Alesina et al. (2004) find that the opposite generally holds true in the European context wherein the inequality effect is driven by the poor becoming unhappy with increased inequality. Additionally, the researchers believe that the results relate to perceptions of social mobility, as Europeans, in general, tend to believe that their chances of moving up the income ladder are low. Once again, it is necessary to emphasize that even if the health of the poor is not negatively affected by inequality per se, they may still be negatively affected by being poor. There is a large strand of literature establishing the consequences of being poor in an absolute sense – both with respect to health but also in regard to other aspects of welfare and life.

7.5   CROSS-COUNTRY STUDIES OF THE INEQUALITY EFFECT

A limitation of studying the inequality hypothesis in a single country is that the results do not necessarily say anything about the situation in other countries or contexts. A number of country-specific circumstances might influence the correlation between inequality and individual health, preventing meaningful generalizations of results. Furthermore, variation in the degree of income inequality across regions within countries is relatively low – a fact that makes it more difficult to identify a statistically significant inequality effect. In other words, there is a risk that the inequality effect is underestimated in country-specific studies.

In recent years, a number of studies comparing individuals in several countries have been published in scientific journals. These studies are largely the result of ambitious data collection projects and supranational initiatives by international organizations (for example, the WHO, 2007 and the EU, 2005). Thus, scholars today have access to comparative data sets containing information about the health of individuals across a number of countries and, in some cases, even over time.

The first analysis using individual data from several countries (Bobak et al., 2000) makes use of information from seven countries in Central and Eastern Europe. This study finds no evidence that within-country (national-level) income inequality has a negative impact on individuals' health after controlling for household incomes and other individual characteristics. Similarly, using data on individuals from 28 European countries in 2003, Zagorski et al. (2014) suggest that the national level of inequality as measured by the Gini coefficient has no statistically significant effect on self-rated health, happiness or life satisfaction. Consequently, these studies also support Gravelle's (1998) critique of Wilkinson's hypothesized harmful effects of inequality.

However, the picture that emerges from studies using data from several countries is not conclusive. Holstein et al. (2009) observe a significant negative correlation between national-level inequality and adolescents' self-reported frequency of various ailments such as headaches, stomach pain and anxiety. It should be noted that, according to this study, there are no indications that the national level of income matters at all. Holstein et al. (2009) use information for more than 200,000 respondents from 37 European and North American countries and adjust for the age and gender of adolescents, as well as for the level of the family wealth based on questions about assets and vacation habits.[10]

A specific measurement problem that becomes pressing when using individual data from a number of countries is that differences in self-reported health may partially reflect national differences in norms and expectations (Sadana et al., 2000). If these cultural differences are correlated with the degree of income inequality, then a statistical analysis may generate inaccurate and misleading results. Karlsson et al. (2010) attempt to address this source of bias in a study that analyses the association between income inequality at the country level and health outcomes using cross-sectional data for individuals residing in 21 countries. They find no evidence consistent with the IIH for the entire cross-sectional sample after controlling for the respondents' age, gender and marital status. However, when they solely focus on individuals living in high-income countries, the analysis indicates a significant negative correlation between inequality and poor self-rated health.

Two more studies evaluate the IIH using individual data from a number of countries over a couple of years. Hildebrand and Van Kerm (2009) investigate the relationship by tracking individuals in 11 EU countries over six years. Like Mellor and Milyo

---

[10] This study therefore suffers from the same problems as Oshio and Kobayashi (2010) (see footnote 7, this chapter), as it does not fully control for differences in household or individual income but rather lets the income variable be categorical. It is difficult to determine how serious this problem really is, and it depends on the research question. For those of us who are primarily interested in how much individual health depends on individual incomes and standards of living – and how much individual health depends on dispersion in the societal income distribution – it is a fairly large problem that income is not measured or evaluated as a continuous variable.

(2002, 2003), they try to account for the possibility that there are non-observable differences across geographical regions that might influence the results. The study finds evidence that an increase in within-country and regional income inequality have negative effects on individual self-reported health, although the magnitudes of the negative effects are small.

This result, however, is challenged by the findings of Jen et al. (2009) who use individual-level data on self-rated health and life satisfaction from 69 countries collected on four occasions over the 1981–2001 period. Contrary to the panel data used by Hildebrand and Van Kerm (2009), the same individuals are not followed over time in this study; rather, the data are repeated cross-sections. Jen et al. (2009) do not find support for the IIH when all 69 countries are analysed at the same time: there is no significant correlation between inequality and health. Moreover, contrary to Karlsson et al. (2010), in relatively rich countries, Jen et al. (2009) find that individuals in unequal countries tend to rate their health more highly than individuals residing in countries that are more equal.[11]

The results of cross-country studies that use happiness and life-satisfaction variables as measure of health are also mixed. On the one hand, Fahey and Smyth (2004) find evidence of the income inequality effect in their study of individuals in 33 European countries. Alesina et al. (2004) also observe a negative correlation between income inequality and happiness among Europeans. These findings also receive support from a recent study of 14 European countries by Cooper et al. (2013), where income inequality is found to have an adverse effect on the subjective well-being of individuals across the whole income distribution, but the poorest individuals are disproportionally affected. Taking a broader geographic focus, Verme (2011) finds an overall negative relationship between inequality and life satisfaction in a study of individuals residing in 84 countries across the globe.

On the other hand, Bjørnskov et al. (2008) use data for approximately 90,000 individuals residing in 70 countries and do not find

---

[11] This study was criticized by Barford et al. (2010). The primary objection raised is the use of self-reported health to study this relationship in several countries at the same time. This type of health measure is likely affected by cultural, historical and institutional factors that, in turn, can influence the correlation between inequality and individual health.

income inequality to be robustly related to life satisfaction. Testing this hypothesis using a sample of individuals from 42 countries, Haller and Hadler (2006) note that greater income inequality tends to make people happier rather than the other way around. In addition, Rözer and Kraaykamp (2013) use data from 85 countries collected between 1989 and 2008 to identify a positive relationship. Their findings indicate that people living in countries that are more unequal report higher happiness and well-being than do people from more equal countries. Dolan et al. (2008) argue that one explanation for the ambiguous evidence reported in the empirical literature on happiness using international data is that the results are easily influenced by the context of each country. Specifically, people living in some countries in Latin America – which generally have large differences in income – tend to be very happy, whereas the level of happiness is generally low in formerly communist countries, even though they are relatively equal.

7.6 STUDIES OF THE RELATIVE INCOME HYPOTHESIS

In Chapter 6, we discussed the RIH as a closely related variant of the IIH of how income differences affect an individual's health. In this section, we survey studies that examine whether an income increase in an individual's reference group has a negative effect on health – holding the income of the individual constant – as suggested by the RIH. If the magnitude of the negative effect on individual health caused by the increased income of the reference group corresponds to the magnitude of the positive effect of the individual's absolute income, then doubling everyone's income would leave mortality unchanged (Gerdtham and Johannesson, 2004).

A few studies have as their primary aim the evaluation of the role of relative income as a determinant of health (see, for example, Yngwe et al., 2003, 2005). However, some of the most recent studies examining the inequality effect also test the RIH. The picture that emerges from this small body of literature is ambiguous, and it is difficult to draw general conclusions.

Among the studies supporting a relative income effect is Luttmer (2005), an extensive US study of how people's health is affected when the income of their neighbours increases. The results hold even after taking individual characteristics or individual fixed effects into consideration. Likewise, Clark (2003) observes a negative effect on individual mental health when people of the same sex earn more income. Karlsson et al. (2010) examine data on individuals in 21 countries and find support for the hypothesis that interpersonal income comparisons have a negative impact on self-reported health. However, their results also indicate that the individual's reference group (or the mechanisms involved) depend on the country's level of economic development. The relative income effect is confirmed in high-income countries when individuals compare themselves with others of their own age. Geographical reference groups, by contrast, are more important in less-developed countries, which may be related to access to information.

In studies using Scandinavian data, Yngwe et al. (2003, 2005) examine the health status of people who belong to the same reference group but have different incomes. The researchers find that individuals with relatively low incomes in their reference groups have significantly lower levels of health, confirming the relative income effect. Having said this, we think that the results should be interpreted carefully: the reference groups are quite widely defined (occupation/socioeconomic group, level of income, age, marital status, country of birth, region of residence), and this specificity can be a source of errors. Furthermore, the authors make no adjustments for the fact that variables are endogenously determined (that is, that health can influence income or that another overlooked or unobserved variable can influence both). This, as we discussed in Chapter 5, can also generate misleading results.

At the other end of the spectrum, a few studies find that the income of the reference group positively affects health. For example, both Miller and Paxson (2006) and Gerdtham and Johannesson (2004) conclude that an increase in the average income of the chosen reference group is related to improved health outcomes in the USA and in Sweden, respectively. Gerdtham and Johannesson (2004) find a statistically significant correlation when average income is measured at the level of Swedish municipalities. Using other geographical reference groups, the correlation with mortality disappears. Miller and Paxson (2006) assume that people compare themselves to people of the same age or ethnicity. It should be noted that both of these studies use objective health measures (risk of mortality) rather than subjective measures. To explain the positive health effect of reference group income, Miller and Paxson (2006) suggest that the average level of income is correlated with factors that may be beneficial for individual health, such as access to health care or to an improved environment (Miller and Paxson, 2006).

The relative income effect has also been examined in happiness research. A clear majority of the studies of rich countries conclude that individual happiness decreases as the income of others increases (for example, Blanchflower and Oswald, 2004; Ferrer-i-Carbonell and Frijters, 2004; Luttmer, 2005). Interestingly, the relationship seems to be the reverse in transitional countries (for example, Senik, 2004; Becchetti and Savastano, 2010). The presence of health benefits in a setting with large relative income differences may be explained by individuals who note that when their peers attain better economic positions they feel better, although their own situations remain unchanged, as the income change of their peers creates an expectation that they will experience a better situation in the near future. This line of reasoning is consistent with Hirschman's (1973) tunnel effect.

Overall, the evidence regarding the RIH is mixed, suggesting that relative changes in income can have both positive and negative effects on individual health. One possibility is that these are countervailing in some cases. For example, no significant correlation between average income and self-reported health is observed in the UK in the examination undertaken by Lorgelly and Lindley (2008). The results indicate that the average incomes of three reference groups, defined by geographical areas, do not influence the health status of the individual, even when his or her income is insignificantly related to health. Furthermore, Hildebrand and Van Kerm (2009) do not find clear support for the relative income effect in a pan-European context. These results are sensitive to the choice of a national or regional reference group and to the consideration of geographical differences in norms. Similar conclusions can be drawn from the work of Soobader and LeClere (1999) as well as Milyo and Mellor (1999), wherein the RIH is evaluated in the US context.

7.7   CONCLUSION: WHAT DOES THE EXISTING RESEARCH TELL US?

In this chapter, we have summarized what we believe to be the most relevant body of literature on the relationship between income inequality and health. We have focused on studies that combine individual and household data with income inequality across a number of regions and countries. As we have tried to show in Chapters 4 to 6, the individual level of analysis is a prerequisite if we want to be able to differentiate among the various mechanisms linking poor health, income and income inequality. Given the limited number of studies using data from developing countries, we mainly focus on studies conducted in relatively rich countries. To ensure quality, we have also limited ourselves to studies that are published in peer-reviewed scientific journals. Finally, we have made an effort to include research from many academic disciplines that contribute to this body of literature.

As a rough overview of all results, we have classified the studies of the IIH into four categories: those that find an unambiguous negative relationship between inequality and health outcomes, those that find some evidence of such a link (such as a negative health effect for a sub-sample but not for the entire population), those that find no significant effect, and those that find that inequality correlates with better health (for either the population or for sub-samples). The results are shown in Figure 7.1.[12]

As indicated in Figure 7.1 there is considerable variation in findings across the studies examined. Despite this variation, there are some patterns worth noting:

- Evidence of an inequality effect is strongest for self-assessed health (SAH): 25 of 43 studies find some negative effect of inequality on health.
- Evidence of an inequality effect on mortality is weak: three of 12 studies find a negative effect, eight studies find no effect, and one study finds some evidence of a positive effect.
- Studies using happiness as the outcome variable produce particularly mixed results, but a negative correlation with inequality is still the most common result.

Based on Figure 7.1, two interpretations are possible. On the one hand, there seems to be considerable evidence of an inequality effect for at least some subjective health measures, although some studies using objective health measures also find an effect. If the link occurs

---

[12] When studies examine several health outcomes, such as self-assessed health and some objective condition, they are counted as two studies.

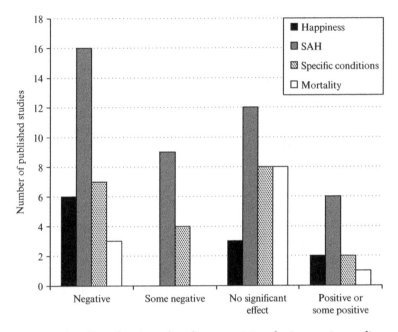

*Figure 7.1   Classification of studies examining the income inequality
hypothesis*

from inequality to health via stress, it is plausible that subjective
health measures are more sensitive than objective measures. On
the other hand, even for subjective health measures, unambiguous
support for inequality effect appears only in a minority of the studies
(16 of 43). According to the hypothesis, inequality negatively affects
the health of the entire population, and thus, studies that find an
effect only for sub-samples of the population should not be viewed
as supportive of this hypothesis.

Are there any patterns beyond what can be seen in Figure 7.1?
For objective health measures, very few find that income inequality
is a significant risk factor for poor health. This result is particularly
clear in rich countries (apart from a study for Norway and one study
for the USA), whereas there is some evidence of an inequality effect
in middle-income countries such as China, Brazil and India. This
difference is interesting considering the number of aggregate studies
focusing on objective health measures, which generally find a strong

negative correlation between inequality and population health (see, for instance, Pampel and Pillai (1986), child mortality; Duleep (1995), adult mortality; Pickett et al. (2005), obesity). The question then arises of whether the results of these population studies are still valid after correcting for individual income. There is no indication that they are.

Looking at studies using subjective, self-assessed health, the picture is different, and several studies find support for an inequality effect. Such evidence often appears in studies of federal inequality and individual health in the USA, while studies of other countries do not arrive at similarly clear-cut conclusions (see, for example, Gravelle and Sutton (2009), the UK; Lorgelly and Lindley (2008), the UK; Shibuya et al. (2002), Japan). The inequality effect on self-reported health is sensitive to accounting for non-observable differences among federal states (see, for example, Mellor and Milyo, 2003). In other words, other variables besides income inequality may drive the negative correlation. One possible alternative explanation is that the level of generalized trust, or social capital, is what matters most. However, in that case, the inequality effect on health should be stronger when income differences are measured close to people's homes rather than when they reflect a large geographical area with many inhabitants.[13] This pattern is not noted in the literature, however. It is perhaps more likely that income inequality affects people's health through purely economic factors originating from various political outcomes (such as public health care). These material factors would then be more important than psychosocial factors, which are also emphasized by the results of Wagstaff and van Doorslaer (2000).

That the results appear to differ between the USA and European countries has led to a discussion about whether it is to be expected that the results should be different in these contexts. Some scholars note that European societies are generally more equal than the USA and, accordingly, that there may be a threshold effect. That is, inequality may only be detrimental to individual health when it exceeds a certain critical value or threshold (Shibuya et al., 2002;

---

[13] Wilkinson and Pickett (2006), however, argue that income inequality manifested in a smaller geographical area most likely does not properly reflect the level of inequality that actually exists in society as a whole and, therefore, that inequality at smaller geographical levels has a lower probability of correlating with health.

Subramanian and Kawachi, 2004). The overall picture emerging from the more recent empirical literature is less consistent with this hypothesis. For example, the inequality effect is not confirmed by studies focusing on the UK or Australia, where regional inequality is comparable to that of the USA.[14] However, Wang et al. (2015) note that individual happiness first increases with rising county-level inequality and then decreases with very high levels of inequality (Gini above 0.405) in China.

Two additional critical observations have materialised during our reading. The first is that remarkably few studies offer conceptual frameworks for setting up and interpreting analyses of the relationship between inequality and individual health.[15] What are the mechanisms that might explain such a link? Perhaps because of this lack of theory, studies differ greatly in their use of controls and inclusion of confounding factors, as well as the measures of health, individual income and inequality that they include in their models. While some studies make adjustments for several individual characteristics (for example, education, job market status, number of people in the household), other studies control only for age and gender. In fact, these model differences may provide partial explanations for the considerable variation in results regarding the inequality effect. We therefore recommend future studies to be more ambitious in specifying the theoretical relationship of interest and identifying possible mechanisms driving the effect of inequality on people's health. Doing this more often would surely produce more succinct results and a better overall understanding of the issue at hand.

Second, very few studies offer a proper statistical identification strategy that allows the authors to make causal interpretations of their results. Some articles mention this limitation but, in many cases, there is a lack of caution in framing the results. Perhaps related to this limitation, few articles discuss the size of their estimated effects. Without such assessments, as we showed in Chapter 6, it is difficult to evaluate the importance of any claimed effects of inequality on people's health or other socially relevant outcomes.

---

[14]   The regional Gini coefficients in Gravelle and Sutton (2009) are around 0.45, which is not dramatically different from the average inequality level in the USA, where the coefficients reached 0.49.
[15]   Notable exceptions include some recent studies on inequality, social capital and individual health (see, for example, Ichida et al., 2009; Aida et al., 2011).

8. Searching for the inequality effect: which tools are appropriate?

One of the main conclusions of our survey of the empirical literature in Chapter 7 is that there is no uniform effect of inequality on individual health. In the cases when such an effect is found to exist, it seems to be contingent on various factors. One of these is the selected inequality measure. In this chapter, we discuss how and why the measurement of inequality dimensions can affect the interpretation of the results in this literature.

Our review of the current research in the previous chapter showed that a large majority of the studies in this field use the Gini coefficient as a statistical measure of income inequality. This measure indeed has a number of tractable theoretical and empirical features, but most reviewed studies do not seem to have chosen it based on an informed discussion of the mechanisms involved or the best way to capture the type of inequality that is expected to be at work. On the contrary, it is our impression that the Gini coefficient is often selected as the inequality measure for conventional reasons rather than because it is the most appropriate measure for a specific context. As we argue in this chapter, an unreflective use of the Gini coefficient risks not only missing important variation in the data but may also add to the confusion of interpreting the results in the literature.

A well-known property of the Gini coefficient is that it does not uniquely identify a particular income distribution. Because the Lorenz curves that underlie the Gini coefficients (see Chapter 3) for different distributions may intersect, an increase in the Gini does not contain information about how and where in the income distribution this change has occurred.[1]

---

[1]   When Lorenz curves intersect, this means that there is no unambiguous ordering of income distributions whatever the class of social welfare functions.

Had theoretical foundations of the inequality effect on health suggested that all types of increasing inequality are equally bad for health, then the interpretation of an increasing Gini coefficient would always be straightforward. However, this is not the case, and several of the relevant theoretical mechanisms that might account for an inequality effect (discussed in detail in Chapter 4) suggest that it actually does matter how the distributional change occurred: does inequality increase mainly because of rising top incomes, increasing dispersion over the entire distribution or deepening poverty? Let us once again review the five mechanisms – social comparisons, social trust, political mechanisms, violence and crime, and inequality and purchasing power – to understand the importance of using the correct measure of inequality, regardless of whether it is the Gini coefficient, top income share or another inequality measure.

8.1   SOCIAL COMPARISONS

One mechanism stresses that social comparisons can affect personal health. If low-income earners compare themselves to other low-income earners and to middle-income earners more often than to high-income earners, then increasing dispersion between the poor and middle-income groups is arguably worse for their health than are increasing top incomes. If, however, people mainly compare themselves to the richest segment, or sports or music superstars earning very high incomes, then raising top incomes would be equally bad. There is a growing literature on peer groups that seeks to identify who we actually compare ourselves to, with some interesting results emerging from various academic disciplines (see, for example, Goldthorpe, 2010; Deaton, 2003). However, there is no clear consensus on what or who constitutes a 'natural peer' and, thus, there is no clear indication of where we should look for the inequality that is expected to most affect health.

8.2   SOCIAL TRUST

A second mechanism is that inequality lowers trust in society, which in turn makes people mistrustful of each other and less reliant on common welfare systems. A negative correlation between inequality and social trust is well documented but, according to Gustavsson and Jordahl (2008), some inequalities are more harmful than others. Differences in the bottom half of the income distribution are more closely associated to lower trust. Again, the mechanism suggests that increasing dispersion over the entire distribution and increasing dispersion in the left tail or in the middle class are worse than increasing top incomes. Recently, however, Barone and Mocetti (2016) have found some (tentative) evidence that changes at the top of the distribution exert the primary impact on the relationship between inequality and trust. Although there may be some ambiguity about where in the distribution the effects are strongest, the overall message – that one may need to consider different parts of the distribution – holds.

8.3 POLITICAL MECHANISMS

Another mechanism emphasizes that distributional outcomes can influence policy making, which in turn generates health effects. If the political mechanisms operate mainly through the median voter (Downs, 1957; Black, 1958), the implications for health will depend on how increasing inequality changes the median income. Increasing top incomes, by definition, do not affect the median income, but the median income is likely affected when the entire income distribution becomes more dispersed. However, if different political mechanisms operate through rent seeking and corruption, increasing top incomes may very well be the most problematic type of inequality from a health perspective.

8.4 VIOLENCE AND CRIME

Another mechanism is that violence and crime make people unhealthy through increased fear and worry as well as through direct acts of violence. According to the famous analysis by Becker (1968), crime can be thought of as the result of the individual choice to engage in criminal activities by comparing the expected returns from crime to the returns from non-criminal activities. This may lead to the conclusion that higher top incomes *ceteris paribus* increase crime, but if increasing top incomes also mean that more money is spent on crime deterrence, the effect is ambiguous. Another implication of the

Becker model is that the cost of committing crimes increases with the potential legal income of the criminal due to the opportunity cost of time. As a result, poverty and unemployment should be associated with more crime. This result is obtained in several empirical studies. For example, Nilsson (2004) finds a link between property crime and the proportion of the population with an income below 10 per cent of the median income. For robbery, a significant effect is found for relative poverty at 10 per cent of the median income, a smaller and less significant effect for relative poverty at 20 per cent of the median, and no effect is found when the poverty line is set at 40 per cent of the median. Nilsson also finds a link between the unemployment rate and overall crime. In contrast, the Gini coefficient and the 90/10 ratio are uncorrelated with the crime rate.[2]

Surveying 17 recent studies on the link between inequality and crime, Rufrancos et al. (2013) conclude that property crime is generally influenced by changing levels of income inequality over time, while the picture is mixed for total violent crime. They also note that the Gini coefficient is by far the most common inequality measure used in studies on the link between inequality and crime, making it difficult to draw conclusions about the exact mechanisms involved.

A particularly interesting paper by Dahlberg and Gustavsson (2008) separates the effect of changes in permanent income from changes in transitory income. While inequality of permanent income increases total crime and three categories of property crimes, inequality in transitory income has no significant effect on crime.

8.5 INEQUALITY AND PURCHASING POWER

Finally, the purchasing power that a given income provides depends on the price structure of the economy, and can affect how people consume and, ultimately, how they feel (Pendakur 2002; Broda et al. 2009; Bergh and Nilsson 2014). Intuitively, when there are more rich people in a society, production will be aimed towards high-income earners. Products aimed at low-income segments will be produced in lower volumes, which means higher prices if economies of scale are not fully utilized, or they may not be produced at all. However,

---

[2]   On the link between unemployment and crime, see Oster and Agell (2007).

a larger segment of low-income earners also implies that selling low-price goods becomes more profitable, affecting the price structure to the benefit of low-income earners (the mechanism is sometimes called the *Walmart effect*).

For a given income difference between the rich and the poor, the purchasing power of the poor is likely to be higher when the poor segment of the market is larger (see Bergh and Nilsson (2013) for empirical evidence). Theoretically, it is thus possible that as the number of poor in a society grows, the purchasing power of the poor increases. The more empirically relevant conclusion, however, is that increasing dispersion of the distribution is likely to be worse for population health than an increase in top incomes in this case.

Consider now the following simple numerical example, where the income distribution in a society with three individuals initially corresponding to {1, 2, 3} changes to {1, 1, 4}. From the definition of the Gini coefficient, inequality can be calculated as follows when the individual incomes are ordered from lowest to highest: y_i, $i = 1$ to n

$$G = \frac{1}{n}(n + 1 - 2)\left(\frac{\sum_{i=1}^{n}(n+1-i)y_i}{\sum_{i=1}^{n}(y_i)}\right)$$

The Gini coefficient increases from 0.22 to 0.33 after this change. At the same time, the difference between the poor and the median decreases, which might mitigate the negative health effects operating through the social comparisons and social trust channels. In addition, the median income earner in the second distribution is poorer (it decreases from 2 to 1), suggesting that policy will be more responsive to the interests of low-income earners. Finally, the market for products aimed at low-income earners grows in the latter setting, suggesting that some adverse effects of earning a low income are mitigated by the purchasing-power effect.

In contrast, if the distribution {1, 2, 3} changes to {1, 3, 6} or even {1, 5, 8}, the increase in the Gini coefficient is the same, but in these cases, all four mechanisms and the purchasing-power effect suggest that individual health outcomes will be adversely affected (controlling for individual income).

The complete numerical example summarized in Table 8.1, illustrates how potentially relevant information for our purposes is lost when using only the Gini coefficient to measure inequality. If the trust and purchasing-power effects are important, the poverty

Table 8.1 Different inequality measures for four hypothetical distributions

Income distribution {poor, median, rich}	Gini	Poverty gap[i]	Median/ mean	Rich/mean
{1, 2, 3}	0.22	0.2	100%	1.5
{1, 1, 4}	0.33	0	50%	2
{1, 3, 6}	0.33	0.8	90%	1.8
{1, 5, 8}	0.33	2	107%	1.7

[i] The poverty gap here corresponds to the difference between the income of the poor and 60 per cent of the median income.

gap might be a suitable measure. If political mechanisms operating through the median voter theorem are important, then the relative income of the median voter is the variable of interest. When the political influence of high-income earners is of interest, top income measures are adequate. As shown in Table 8.1, these indicators can vary substantially, even for distributions for which the Gini coefficient does not vary.

8.6 SUMMING UP

The fact that the Gini coefficient has become the focal point in most studies of the relationship between inequality and individual health is both a blessing and a curse.

On the blessing side, the use of a recognized and well-behaved inequality measure is positive, and when several studies use it, they create comparable results. This requires, however, that comparable Gini coefficients are used, and closer scrutiny reveals that many studies lack clarity regarding the use of household, individual or tax units to calculate inequality. The same is true for income concepts (which can include, for example, disposable income, wage income or expenditures). As we highlighted in Chapter 3, it is critical that one selects inequality data that is comparable across countries and over time, depending on the context of the investigation.[3]

---

[3] There are a few cross-national data sets providing measures of income inequality,

On the curse side, even when Gini coefficients are clearly defined and comparable, they do not tell us very much about dynamics within different parts of the income distribution. Studies searching for an inequality effect on health using only the Gini therefore run the risk of missing the important variation if the effects are only visible in some parts of the population. In this case, the use of a measure that is *motivated by the theoretical mechanisms* may lead to significant results. Conversely, significant findings in studies using the Gini are less convincing than they would have been because the Gini coefficient does not always pick up the changes that matter while picking up changes that theoretically do not matter.

Choosing the measure of inequality with care is important in light of the results in Jones and Wildman (2008), which show that the health-income gradient exhibits considerable irregularity at the lower end of the income distribution. This could be interpreted as another causal relationship from health to income. It is therefore reasonable to believe that findings for the inequality effect may also be affected by how much weight the inequality measure assigns to different segments of the income distribution.

Our recommendation is that studies of the inequality effect on health should first define the relevant mechanism or mechanisms and determine how they can be detected empirically. Only then should the researcher select an appropriate measure that is able to capture these potential distributional outcomes, be it the poverty rate, top income share or, perhaps, the Gini coefficient.

---

all of which have their own advantages and disadvantages, for example, the World Income Inequality Database (WIID), the Luxembourg Income Study (LIS), the World Top Income Database (WTID) and the Standardized World Income Inequality Database SWIID (see, for example, Atkinson and Brandolini, 2001; Solt, 2009, 2016; Jenkins, 2015).

9. Conclusion

In 2001, a reputable scientific journal, *Annals of Internal Medicine*, published an article with a sensational result: actors who have ever won an Oscar live four years longer than other actors (Redelmeier and Singh, 2001). The article built on many observations structured such that winners were compared with other actors of the same gender, age and who had acted in the same movie. The result was statistically significant, and the positive effect on longevity of four years was large. Besides Oscar glory, living for four more years because of an elevation in status is not a bad reward. This finding was quickly acknowledged and offered as an example of how our tendency to compare ourselves with others affects our well-being.[1]

There is only one problem: the result later turned out to be flawed. The researchers had made the relatively simple methodological error of comparing the longevity of Oscar winners without considering the fact that these actors were relatively old when they were honoured and were therefore even more likely to reach an older age. A statistician would say that life expectancy for someone who is alive, for example, at age 60 is higher than their life expectancy at birth. This methodological mistake gave the Oscar winners an unfair advantage in the comparison, and when other researchers accounted for this age effect, the positive effect of status on health disappeared.[2] Despite the invalidation of this finding, it remains a common reference, particularly in media but also in scientific work.

This episode is illuminating in several ways. It shows that even professional scholars can make methodological mistakes. It also shows how sensational results tend to be tested and examined more closely by other scholars. This means that results that last can be

---

[1] One prominent example is Michael Marmot's book *The Status Syndrome* (2004).

[2] This mistake (so-called mortality bias) was identified in an article published in 2006 – five years after the initial article. A corrected statistical analysis showed that the difference in longevity between Oscar winners and other actors is not statistically significant (at a 95% confidence level). See Sylvestre et al. (2006).

separated from those that result from mistakes or unlikely coincidences. A third thing we can learn from this episode is that unexpected and exciting results can quickly reach many people, even after they have proved flawed.

There are many parallels between the above story and the previous discussion of the effect of inequality on health. As we show in this book, it is easy to present data such that it seems to confirm the inequality effect. After all, numerous studies using aggregate population data find a negative association between inequality and average population health. The notion that the level of variation in the distribution of income would significantly affect people's health is suggestive, exciting and politically controversial, and it is not surprising that this idea has spread far beyond the pages of academic journals.

However, as this book also shows, scatter plots and aggregate-level correlations provide insufficient evidence of whether income differences make us sick. For a study to be able to say anything about how much of a person's health depends on their income – and how much depends on income distribution in society – it has to use individual or household data as well as data on the overall income distribution.

We reviewed studies using individual-level data, and their empirical findings are not as clear-cut as those produced by earlier studies using aggregate data. We have, however, detected some noticeable patterns.

First, studies using individual data strongly support the notion that the level of income matters for health, which is in line with the absolute income hypothesis (AIH). Even in rich countries, such as the UK or France, where most people have high incomes, there is generally a positive correlation at the individual level between income and health. As we have noted, however, this correlation might actually stem from higher incomes, leading to better health, and from the fact that healthy people are able to work more and therefore earn more money.

Second, the income inequality hypothesis (IIH) – that is, the conjecture that people living in rich, unequal countries have worse health than people living in rich, equal countries – is not strongly supported by the data. It cannot, however, be dismissed as wrong. Among the 87 surveyed studies that use individual data, 45 find some evidence of a negative inequality effect; 31 studies do not find any significant or find very mixed results, whereas 11 studies find a positive correlation between inequality and health.[3] The claim that the inequality effect, if found, should primarily exist in rich countries has no clear support in the literature. There are rich countries for which the effect is not found, and there are poor countries where it is encountered. Studies using subjective health measures are overrepresented among studies that find significant inequality effects, whereas studies using objective health measures typically find no support.[4] Support for the notion that subjective wellbeing suffers due to societal differences in income thus seems stronger than the support for the notion that we get physically sick from such differences.

Third, our survey shows that studies rarely discuss the magnitudes of estimated health effects. This is problematic because policy makers always need to weigh the costs and benefits of all the political measures at their disposal. For illustrative purposes, let us consider how this could be done using the results reported in Karlsson et al. (2010), a study of longitudinal individual data for several countries that observed an inequality effect for rich countries using self-assessed health (but not for middle-income countries or for more objective health outcomes).[5] The magnitude of this inequality effect is not large: if one of the most unequal developed countries, the UK, was to reduce its level of inequality to the same level as the most equal country, Denmark (a Gini decrease from 34 to 24), this would raise the share of Britons self-reporting their health at the highest (best) level from 47 per cent to 52 per cent. This calculation is built on the assumption that inequality in the UK could be reduced to the level of Denmark without influencing any other factors that affect health. This is not very likely considering the magnitude of such a

---

[3] A similar conclusion is reached in another survey on the research in this multifaceted field, namely, that the results do not show a clear inequality effect. However, few studies have managed to convincingly show that the effect *does not* exist (Leigh et al., 2009, p. 399).

[4] Only four studies using objective health measure support the inequality hypothesis: Dahl et al. (2006) on mortality in Norway; Li and Zhu (2006) on heart problems (but not blood pressure) in China; Lochner et al. (2001) on mortality in the USA; and Subramanian et al. (2007) on being over- or underweight among married or divorced women in India.

[5] Please note that in order to illustrate the size of the inequality effect, we chose a study that actually finds an inequality effect, that we chose a health measure and a selection of countries in this study where the effect appears, and, finally, that we assume that the effect can be interpreted as causal relationship.

societal change. Still, Karlsson et al. (2010) note that the size of their estimated effect is 'considerable' in comparison to the similar study by Hildebrand and Van Kerm (2009).

Moreover, Karlsson et al. (2010) also find that household income is statistically significantly related to health, for both objective and subjective health and that the effect is greater for low-income earners (just as illustrated in Figure 6.1). According to the estimates in Karlsson et al. (2010), the health benefits associated with reducing the country-level Gini coefficient from 34 to 24 is equivalent to raising adjusted annual household income by \$10,000 (more for high-income households and less for low-income households due to the non-linear relationship between income and health). In other words, political measures aiming to increase the income of the poorest stand a good chance at improving their health.

Even if one chooses to fully believe the results of studies that find support for the inequality effect, the fact remains that societal income distributions change very slowly. There are good reasons to strive for equal distributions of incomes and health, but it is still difficult to scientifically establish how they are interrelated.

Appendix

Studies using individual level data for multiple countries

Article	Period	Countries	Measure of inequality	Geographical aggregation level	Health measure	Results	RIH	Comment
Alesina et al. (2004)	1975–1992	12 EU countries and USA	Gini	National (state level for the US)	Happiness	Inequality (−) In the USA, the effect is larger for rich individuals; in the EU, the effect is larger for poor individuals		Panel for macro variables, but pooled individual level data
Bobak et al. (2000)	1996, 1997 and 1998	7 Central- and Eastern European countries	Gini	National	SAH	Inequality (0)		
Cooper et al. (2013)	1994–2001	14 European countries	Gini; Theil, Kakwani, P90/P10 ratio, standard deviation of logarithms	National	Subjective well-being	Inequality (−)		Household-equalized net income Income inequality seem to have a more adverse impact on the poor

Study	Years	Sample	Inequality measure	Level	Outcome	Result	Other
Fahey and Smyth (2004)	1999–2000	33 European countries	Gini (1990)	National	Happiness	Inequality (−)	
Haller and Hadler (2006)	1995–1997	41 countries	Gini	National	Happiness	Inequality (+)	
Hildebrand and Van Kerm (2009)	1996–2001	11 EU-15 countries	Gini, P90/P10 ratio, GE, coefficient of variation	National (11), regions (52)	SAH	Inequality (−)	Relative income (0)
Holstein et al. (2009)	2005–2006	37 countries	Gini	National	Self-reported ailments	Inequality (−)	
Jen et al. (2009)	1981, 1991, 1995–1997, 1999–2000	69 countries	Gini	National	SAH	Inequality (0/+)	Categorical income variable Full sample: inequality (0) Rich countries: Inequality (+)

Article	Period	Countries	Measure of inequality	Geographical aggregation level	Health measure	Results	RIH	Comment
Karlsson et al. (2010)	2006	21 countries	Gini	National inequality, national or regional relative income	SAH, activities of daily living (ADL)	Rich countries: Inequality (−) Poor countries: Inequality (0)	Relative income (−), different reference groups are important in rich and poor countries	
Verme (2011)	1981–2004	84 countries	Gini	National	Subjective well-being	Inequality (−)		
Zagorski et al. (2014)	2003	28 European countries	Gini	National	SAH, satisfaction with health	Inequality (0)		

Studies using individual level data for single countries

Article	Time period	Country	Measure of inequality	Geographical aggregation level	Health measure	Results	RIH	Comment
Aida et al. (2011)	2003	Japan	Gini	Local districts (79)	SAH Dental status (nr of teeth)	Inequality (−) Stronger effect for dental status than SAH		Control for social capital
Alesina et al. (2004)	1975– 1992	USA	Gini	State	Happiness	Inequality (−) Result driven by a negative relationship for rich individuals		
Bechtel et al. (2012)	2001– 2008	Australia	Gini, Theil, Atkinson		Mental health	Inequality (0) No support for IIH		
Blakely et al. (2000)	1995, 1997	USA	Gini	State	SAH	Inequality (−)		
Blakely et al. (2002)	1996, 1998	USA	Gini	Metropolitan area, county	SAH	Inequality (0)		Categoric inequality variable
Blakely et al. (2003)	1991, 1994	New Zealand	Gini	Region (35)	Mortality	Inequality (0)		
Blanchflower and Oswald (2004)	1972– 1998	USA		State	Happiness		Relative income (−)	

Article	Time period	Country	Measure of inequality	Geographical aggregation level	Health measure	Results	RIH	Comment
Carlson (2005)	1998	Russia	Gini	Region (39)	SAH	Inequality (0/−) Negative correlation for men. No significant relationship for women		
Chang and Christakis (2005)	1996–1998	USA	Gini, Robin Hood index, coefficient of variation	Metropolitan areas	BMI, obesity	Inequality (0/+) No general inequality effect. Positive correlation for white women		
Chen and Gotway Crawford (2012)	2000	USA	Gini	State, county	Health insurance status Influenza vaccination SAH Obesity	Inequality (−/0/+) Results vary depending on geographical scale and health measure		

Study	Years	Country	Inequality measure	Level (unit)	Outcome	Result	Categorical inequality variable
Chen and Meltzer (2008)	1991, 1993, 1997, 2000	China	Coefficent of variation	Municipalities (190)	Obesity, blood preasure	Inequality (0/−) Confirms IIH in rural, but not urban areas	Catgorical inequality variable
Chiavegatto Filho et al. (2013)	2005–2007 2010	Brazil	Gini	Metropolitan areas of São Paulo Local units (69)	Mental disorder	Inequality (−) Confirm IIH	
Clark (2003)	1996–2001	UK	Gini	Reference group (gender, region)	Happiness	Inequality (+)	
Craig (2005)	1999, 2000	Scotland	Gini, 90/10 ratio, Theils index	Municipality (32)	SAH	Inequality (+)	
Daly et al. (1998)	1978–1982, 1988–1992	USA	Decile ratio, share of total incomes held by the 50% poorest population	State	Mortality	Inequality (0)	
Dahl et al. (2006)	1993, 1999	Norway	Gini	Economic regions (88)	Mortality	Inequality (−) Stronger relationship for poorer individuals	

Article	Time period	Country	Measure of inequality	Geographical aggregation level	Health measure	Results	RIH	Comment
Edvinsson et al. (2013)	2006	Sweden	Gini	Municipalities	Mortality	Inequality (−)		Sample of elderly people, age 65–74
Feng et al. (2012)	2008	China	Gini (2008, 2005, 2002)	Provinces (23) only 22 provinces in lagged ineq.	Self-rated health	Inequality (−) Stronger effect for women and uneducated in unequal areas Support IIH		Sample of elderly people, age 60–112 (younger elders 60–79, oldest-old 80–112) Control for lagged inequality (Gini from 3 years)
Fiscella and Franks (2000)	1982–1984, 1987	USA	P50/total income	County	Mortality, SAH	Inequality – SAH (−) Inequality – mortality (0)		
Fiscella and Franks (1997)	1971–1975, 1987 (död-lighet)	USA	Share of total incomes held by the 50% poorest population	Community	Mortality	Inequality (0)		

Study	Period	Country	Inequality measure	Level (n)	Health measure	Inequality result	Relative income	Notes
Gerdtham and Johannesson (2004)	1980–1986, 1996	Sweden	Gini, Robin Hood index, variance of log income, coefficient of variation	County (24), municipality, labour market area (100)	Mortality	Inequality (0), Neither any significant relationship for poor individuals	Relative income (0/+)	County and labour market area fixed effects
Gravelle and Sutton (2009)	1979–2000	UK	Gini	National, regions (11)	SAH, ALLI (proponged illness)	Inequality (0/+/−)		Regional inequality positively related to health with fixed effects. National inequality negatively related if time trends not included. When time trends included inequality relates positively to health.

Article	Time period	Country	Measure of inequality	Geographical aggregation level	Health measure	Results	RIH	Comment
Grönqvist et al. (2012)	1987–2004 (1990)	Sweden	Gini, Coefficient of variation, Log 90/10 percentile income ratio	Municipality	Hospitalization (sick leave, mortality)	Inequality (0)		Make us of a quasi-experiment (settlement policy) to handle endogeneity problems. Sample include all refugees aged 25–60 who arrived to the country between 1990 and 1994.
Henriksson et al. (2010)	1991–1998	Sweden	Gini	Municipality (41), parishes (729)	Incidents of acute myocardial infarction (AMI)	Inequality (+)		
Ichida et al. (2009)	2003	Japan	Gini	Communities (25)	SAH	Inequality (−)	Inequality (−)	Control for social capital. Sample of individuals

Study	Country	Year	Inequality measure	Level	Health outcome	Results	Notes
Kahn et al. (2000)	USA	1991	Gini	State	SAH, depressive symptoms among mothers	Inequality (−), especially for low-income groups	aged 65 or over. Self-rated health as dichotomous variable Equalized household income (from categorical annual household income data)
Karlsdotter et al. (2012)	Spain	2007	Gini, Thiel, per capita income Atkinson, per capita welfare and welfare loss due to inequality	Region (17)	Self-perceived health Chronic illness	Inequality (0/−) Support for IIH for chronic illness but not for self-preceived health	Categorical income- and inequality variables
Kennedy et al. (1998)	USA	1993	Gini	State	SAH	Inequality (−) Stronger relationship for poorer indviduals	

Article	Time period	Country	Measure of inequality	Geographical aggregation level	Health measure	Results	RIH	Comment
Larrea and Kawachi (2005)	1998	Ecuador	Gini	Municipality area (171), municipality (53), province (19)	Child health (stunting)	Inequality (0/−)		Negative correlation only observed for provinces
LeClere and Soobader (2000)	1989–1991	USA	Gini	County	SAH	Inequality (−) Tthe inequality effect is restricted to certain demographic groups		
Li and Zhu (2006)	1993	China	Gini	Municipality	SAH, objective health outcomes	Inequality (−)		Men and women are statistically more likely to report poorer health if income was more unequally distributed during the first year of their lives

Study	Years	Country	Inequality measure	Level	Outcome	Inequality	Relative income	Controls
Lillard et al. (2015)	1984–2009	USA	Top percentiles	National	SAH	Inequality (−)		
Lochner et al. (2001)		USA	Gini	State	Mortality	Inequality (−)		
Lorgelly and Lindley (2008)	1991–2004	UK	Gini, GE, Atkinson measures	National, regions, counties	SAH	Inequality (0)	Relative income (0)	
Luttmer (2005)	1987–1988, 1992–1994	USA	Gini, average incomes in the area	PUMAS	Happiness	Inequality (0)	Relative income (−)	
Martikainen et al. (2004)	1990, 1991–2001	Finland	Gini	Regions (85)	Suicidal mortality risk	Inequality (0)		
McLeod et al. (2003)	1994	Canada	Share of total incomes held by the 50% poorest population	Metropolitan areas (53)	SAH	Inequality (0)		Controls for social capital
Meara (1999)	1990	USA	Gini, decile ratio, share of total incomes held by the 50% poorest population	State	Child mortality, birth weight	Inequality (0)		

Article	Time period	Country	Measure of inequality	Geographical aggregation level	Health measure	Results	RIH	Comment
Mellor and Milyo (2002)	1995–1999	USA	Coefficient of variation, ratio 90/10, share of income in top half of the distribution	State, metropolitan areas	SAH	The inequality effect disappears when including individual characteristics. No different for poor individuals.		
Mellor and Milyo (2003)	1995–1999	USA	Gini	State	SAH, mortality	Inequality (0)		With no fixed effects the IIH is confirmed, but the effect dissappears when they are included.
Miller and Paxson (2006)	1980, 1990	USA		Reference group (age, gender, race, regions)	Mortality		Relative income (0/+)	Certain dempographic groups, e.g. black men in working age, have a

Study	Country	Period	Inequality measure	Level	Outcome	Result	Notes
							lower mortality risk if they live in relatively rich areas.
Oishi et al. (2011)	USA	1972–2008	Gini	National	Happiness	Inequality (−)	Subjective well-being on a three point happiness item on the GSS
Oshio and Kobayashi (2010)	Japan	2001, 2004, 2007	Gini	Prefectures (47)	SAH, happiness	Inequality (−)	Categorical income variable, pooled data
Osler et al. (2002)	Denmark	1976–1978, 1993–1994	Share of total gross incomes held by the 50% poorest population	City districts	Mortality	Inequality (0)	
Rostila et al. (2012)	Sweden	2002	Gini	Muncipality (25), neighbourhoods (709)	Self-rated health	Inequality (+/0)	No significant effects when focusing on neighborhoods Control for spending on social goods

Article	Time period	Country	Measure of inequality	Geographical aggregation level	Health measure	Results	RIH	Comment
Schwarze and Härpfer (2007)	1985–1998	Germany	Gini, Theil, Atkinson (calculated on gross income)	Regions	Happiness	Inequality (–)		
Senik (2004)	1994–2000	Russia	Gini	Regioners (8), sampling units (100)	Happiness	Inequality (0)	Relative income (+)	
Shi and Starfield (2000)	1996	USA	Gini	State	SAH	Inequality (–)		
Shibya et al. (2002)	1995	Japan	Gini	Prefectures	SAH	Inequality (0)		
Soobader and LeClere (1999)	1989–1991	USA	Gini	Counties	SAH	Inequality (–),		Sample only consists of white men
Sturm and Gresenz (2002)	1997–1998	USA	Gini	Metropolitan areas	Self reported health problems, depression, anxiety	Inequality (0)		
Subramanian and Kawachi (2006)	1995, 1997	USA	Gini	State	SAH	Inequality (–) Stronger effect for richer individuals		

Study	Year	Country	Inequality measure	Level	Outcome	Effect	Comments
Subramanian et al. (2001)	1993–1994	USA	Gini	State	SAH	Inequality (0/+)	No general inequality effect. Rich individuals tend to have better health if they live in unequal states
Subramanian et al. (2003)	2000	Chile	Gini	Municipalities (285)	SAH	Inequality (−)	
Subramanian et al. (2007)	1998–1999	India	Gini	State	Overweight, underweight	Inequality (−)	Inequality increases the risk of both over- and underweight
Tomes (1986)	1977	Canada	Share of total incomes held by the 10% richest population, share of total incomes held by the 40% poorest population	Electoral districts	Happiness	Inequality (0)	

Article	Time period	Country	Measure of inequality	Geographical aggregation level	Health measure	Results	RIH	Comment
Weich et al. (2001)	1991	UK	Gini	Regions	Psychological disorder	Rich individuals: Inequality (−) Poor individuals: Inequality (+)		
Weich et al. (2002)	1991	UK	Gini, GE(0), GE(1), GE(2)	Regions	SAH	Inequality (0/−) Negative relationship for poorer individuals. Results varied with choice of inequality measure		
Wong et al. (2009)	2002, 2005	Hong Kong	Gini	Neighborhoods (287 st)	SAH	Inequality (0) Neither any evidence of an inequality effect for poor individuals		

Study	Years	Country	Inequality measures	Level	Outcome	Finding	Notes
Zhen and George (2012)	1984–2007	USA	Gini, Income ratios: 50/20, 80/50, 95/50, 95/80, 95/20	National	Physical functioning Activity limitation	Inequality (−)	Family income as continous variable and category variable Pooled cross-sectional data
Zheng (2009)	1972–2004	USA	Gini, Thiel, Atkinson	National	Self-rated health	Inequaliy (−) Stronger effect on men's health	Income inequality data from the US Census Bureau
Zheng (2012)	1986, 2004–2006	USA	Gini, Theil, Atkinson	National	Mortality risk	Inequality (−) Long-term effect on increased individual mortality risk	A lagged adverse effect of the Gini coefficient that peaked 7 years later and had effect up to 12 years

Article	Time period	Country	Measure of inequality	Geographical aggregation level	Health measure	Results	RIH	Comment
								A lagged effect with the Theil and Atkinson indexes comes earlier (begin after 3 years and end after 11)

Note: A negative sign always implies that the study notes inequality worsens health, independently of what measure used.

Bibliography

Aaberge, Rolf, Manudeep Singh Bhuller, Audun Langørgen and
Magne Mogstad (2010), 'The distributional impact of public services when needs differ', *Journal of Public Economics*, **94** (9–10),
549–62.

Aida, J., K. Kondo, N. Kondo, R.G. Watt, A. Sheiham and
G. Tsakos (2011), 'Income inequality, social capital and self-rated
health and dental status in older Japanese', *Social Science &
Medicine*, **73** (10), 1561–8.

Alesina, A., R. Di Tella and R. MacCulloch (2004), 'Inequality and
happiness: are Europeans and Americans different?' *Journal of
Public Economics*, **88** (9–10), 2009–42.

Alesina, Alberto, Reza Baqir and William Easterly (1999), 'Public
goods and ethnic divisions', *Quarterly Journal of Economics*, **114**
(4), 1243–84.

Almond, Douglas (2006), 'Is the 1918 influenza pandemic over?
Long-term effects of in utero influenza exposure in the post-1940
US population', *Journal of Political Economy*, **114** (4), 672–712.

Almond, Douglas and Janet Currie (2011), 'Killing me softly: the
fetal origins hypothesis', *Journal of Economic Perspectives*, **25** (3),
153–72.

Almond, Douglas, Lena Edlund and Mårten Palme (2009),
'Chernobyl's subclinical legacy: prenatal exposure to radioactive
fallout and school outcomes in Sweden', *Quarterly Journal of
Economics*, **124** (4), 1729–72.

Araujo, M.C., F.H.G. Ferreira, P. Lanjouw and B. Ozler (2008),
'Local inequality and project choice: theory and evidence from
Ecuador', *Journal of Public Economics*, **92** (5–6), 1022–46.

Atkinson, Anthony B. (1975), *Economics of Inequality*, Oxford:
Oxford University Press.

Atkinson, Anthony B. and Andrea Brandolini (2001), 'Promise and
pitfalls in the use of "secondary" data-sets: income inequality in
OECD countries as a case study', *Journal of Economic Literature*,
39 (3), 771–99.

Babones, S.J. (2008), 'Income inequality and population health: correlation and causality', *Social Science & Medicine*, **66** (7), 1614–26.

Baker, Michael, Mark Stabile and Catherine Deri (2004), 'What do self-reported, objective, measures of health measure?', *Journal of Human Resources*, **39** (4), 1067–93.

Barford, A., D. Dorling and K. Pickett (2010), 'Re-evaluating self-evaluation: a commentary on Jen, Jones, and Johnston (68:4, 2009)', *Social Science & Medicine*, **70** (4), 496–7.

Barone, Guglielmo and Sauro Mocetti (2016), 'Inequality and trust: new evidence from panel data', *Economic Inquiry*, **54** (2), 794–809.

Becchetti, L. and S. Savastano (2010), 'The money-happiness relationship in transition countries: evidence from Albania', *Transition Studies Review*, **17** (1), 39–62.

Bechtel, L., G. Lordan and D.S. Rao (2012), 'Income inequality and mental health – empirical evidence from Australia', *Health Economics*, **21** (Suppl. 1), 4–17.

Becker, Gary S. (1968), 'Crime and punishment: an economic approach', *The Journal of Political Economy*, **76** (2), 169–217.

Bengtsson, Niklas, Bertil Holmlund and Daniel Waldenström (2016), 'Lifetime versus annual tax progressivity: Sweden, 1968–2009', *Scandinavian Journal of Economics*, in press.

Benjamins, M.R., R.A. Hummer, I.W. Eberstein and C.B. Nam (2004), 'Self-reported health and adult mortality risk: an analysis of cause-specific mortality', *Social Science & Medicine*, **59** (6), 1297–306.

Berggren, Niclas and Christian Bjørnskov (2011), 'Is the importance of religion in daily life related to social trust? Cross-country and cross-state comparisons', *Journal of Economic Behavior & Organization*, **80** (3), 459–80.

Bergh, A. (2009), *Den Kapitalistiska Välfärdsstaten*, Stockholm: Norstedts akademiska förlag.

Bergh, A. and C. Bjørnskov (2014), 'Trust, welfare states and income equality: sorting out the causality', *European Journal of Political Economy*, **35**, 183–99.

Bergh, A. and T. Nilsson (2010), 'Good for living? On the relationship between globalization and life expectancy', *World Development*, **38** (9), 1191–203.

Bergh, A. and T. Nilsson (2013), 'When more poor means less poverty: on income inequality and purchasing power', *Southern Economic Journal*, **81** (1), 232–46.

Bergh, A. and T. Nilsson (2014), 'When more poor means less poverty: on income inequality and purchasing power', *Southern Economic Journal*, **81** (1), 232–46.

Björklund, A. (1993), 'A comparison between actual distributions of annual and lifetime income: Sweden 1951–89', *Review of Income and Wealth*, **39** (4), 377–86.

Björklund, A. and M. Jäntti (2011), *Inkomstfördelningen in Sverige, SNS Välfärdsrådets Rapport*, Stockholm: SNS Förlag.

Bjørnskov, C., A. Dreher and J.A. Fischer (2008), 'Cross-country determinants of life satisfaction: exploring different determinants across groups in society', *Social Choice and Welfare*, **30** (1), 119–73.

Black, Duncan (1958), *The Theory of Committees and Elections*, Cambridge: Cambridge University Press.

Black, Sandra E., Paul J. Devereux and Kjell G. Salvanes (2007), 'From the cradle to the labor market? The effect of birth weight on adult outcomes', *The Quarterly Journal of Economics*, **122** (1), 409–39.

Blakely, T., J. Atkinson and D. O'Dea (2003), 'No association of income inequality with adult mortality within New Zealand: a multi-level study of 1.4 million 25–64 year olds', *Journal of Epidemiology and Community Health*, **57** (4), 279–84.

Blakely, T.A., B.P. Kennedy, R. Glass and I. Kawachi (2000), 'What is the lag time between income inequality and health status?' *Journal of Epidemiology and Community Health*, **54** (4), 318–19.

Blakely, T.A., K. Lochner and I. Kawachi (2002), 'Metropolitan area income inequality and self-rated health – a multi-level study', *Social Science and Medicine*, **54** (1), 65–77.

Blanchflower, D.G. and A.J. Oswald (2004), 'Well-being over time in Britain and the USA', *Journal of Public Economics*, **88** (7–8), 1359–86.

Bobak, M., H. Pikhart, R. Rose, C. Hertzman and M. Marmot (2000), 'Socioeconomic factors, material inequalities, and perceived control in self-rated health: cross-sectional data from seven post-communist countries', *Social Science and Medicine*, **51** (9), 1343–50.

Brehm, John and Wendy Rahn (1997), 'Individual-level evidence for the causes and consequences of social capital', *American Journal of Political Science*, **41** (3), 999–1023.

Broda, C., E. Leibtag and David E. Weinstein (2009), 'The role of prices in measuring the poor's living standards', *Journal of Economic Perspectives*, **23** (2), 77–97.

Burkhauser, R.V. and J. Cawley (2008), 'Beyond BMI: the value of more accurate measures of fatness and obesity in social science research', *Journal of Health Economics*, **27** (2), 519–29.

Canning, D. and D. Bowser (2010), 'Investing in health to improve the wellbeing of the disadvantaged: reversing the argument of fair society, healthy lives (the Marmot Review)', *Social Science & Medicine*, **71** (7), 1223–6.

Carlson, P. (2005), 'Relatively poor, absolutely ill? A study of regional income inequality in Russia and its possible health consequences', *Journal of Epidemiology and Community Health*, **59** (5), 389–94.

Case, Anne and Angus S. Deaton (2005), 'Broken down by work and sex: how our health declines', in David A. Wise (ed.), *Analyses in the Economics of Aging*, Chicago: University of Chicago Press, 185–212.

Cesarini, David, E. Lindqvist, R. Ostling and B. Wallace (2016), 'Wealth, health, and child development: evidence from administrative data on Swedish lottery players', *Quarterly Journal of Economics* (in press).

Chan, A., C. Malhotra, Y.K. Do, R. Malhotra and T. Ostbyea (2011), 'Self-reported pain severity among multiethnic older Singaporeans: does adjusting for reporting heterogeneity matter?' *European Journal of Pain*, **15** (10), 1094–9.

Chang, V.W. and N.A. Christakis (2005), 'Income inequality and weight status in US metropolitan areas', *Social Science & Medicine*, **61** (1), 83–96.

Chen, Z. and C.A. Gotway Crawford (2012), 'The role of geographic scale in testing the income inequality hypothesis as an explanation of health disparities', *Social Science & Medicine*, **75** (6), 1022–31.

Chen, Z. and D. Meltzer (2008), 'Beefing up with the Chans: evidence for the effects of relative income and income inequality on health from the China Health and Nutrition Survey', *Social Science & Medicine*, **66** (11), 2206–17.

Chiavegatto Filho, A.D., I. Kawachi, Y.P. Wang, M.C. Viana and L.H. Andrade (2013), 'Does income inequality get under the skin? A multilevel analysis of depression, anxiety and mental disorders in São Paulo, Brazil', *Journal of Epidemiology and Community Health*, **67** (11), 966–72.

Clark, Andrew E. (2003), 'Inequality aversion and income mobility: a direct test', working paper, Centre National de la Reserche Scientifique: DELTA.

Clark, Andrew E. and Claudia Senik (2010), 'Who compares to whom? The anatomy of income comparisons in Europe', *The Economic Journal*, **120** (544), 573–94.

Clark, T. and A. Leicester (2004), 'Inequality and two decades of British tax and benefit reforms', *Fiscal Studies*, **25** (2), 129–58.

Coleman, J.S. (1990), *The Foundations of Social Theory*, Cambridge, MA: Harvard University Press.

Cooper, D., W.D. McCausland and I. Theodossiou (2013), 'Income inequality and wellbeing: the plight of the poor and the curse of permanent inequality', *Journal of Economic Issues*, **47** (4), 939–58.

Cowell, Frank (2011), *Measuring Inequality*, Oxford: Oxford University Press.

Craig, N. (2005), 'Exploring the generalisability of the association between income inequality and self-assessed health', *Social Science & Medicine*, **60** (11), 2477–88.

Creedy, John (1999), 'Lifetime versus annual income distribution', in J. Silber (ed.), *Handbook of Income Inequality Measurement*, Amsterdam: Kluwer Academic Publishing.

Currie, J. and Maya Rossin-Slater (2015), 'Early-life origins of life-cycle well-being: research and policy implications', *Journal of Policy Analysis and Management*, **34** (1), 208–42.

Currie, J. and M. Stabile (eds) (2006), *Mental Health in Childhood and Human Capital*, Chicago: University of Chicago Press.

Dahl, E., J. Ivar Elstad, D. Hofoss and M. Martin-Mollard (2006), 'For whom is income inequality most harmful? A multi-level analysis of income inequality and mortality in Norway', *Social Science and Medicine*, **63** (10), 2562–74.

Dahlberg, Matz and Magnus Gustavsson (2008), 'Inequality and crime: separating the effects of permanent and transitory income', *Oxford Bulletin of Economics and Statistics*, **70** (2), 129–53.

Daly, M.C., G.J. Duncan, G.A. Kaplan and J.W. Lynch (1998), 'Macro-to-micro links in the relation between income inequality and mortality', *The Milbank Quarterly*, **76** (3), 315–39.

Deaton, Angus (2003), 'Health, inequality, and economic development', *Journal of Economic Literature*, **41** (1), 113–58.

Deaton, Angus (2013), *The Great Escape: Health, Wealth, and the Origins of Inequality*, Princeton: Princeton University Press.

Dehejia, R.H. and A. Lleras-Muney (2004), 'Booms, busts, and babies' health', National Bureau of Economics Research.

Di Tella, R. and R. MacCulland (2008), 'Happiness adaptation to income beyond basic needs', NBER working paper no. 14539.

Dolan, P., T. Peasgood and M. White (2008), 'Do we really know what makes us happy? A review of the economic literature on the factors associated with subjective well-being', *Journal of Economic Psychology*, **29** (1), 94–122.

Dowd, J.B. and M. Todd (2011), 'Does self-reported health bias the measurement of health inequalities in US adults? Evidence using anchoring vignettes from the health and retirement study', *Journals of Gerontology Series B: Psychological Sciences and Social Sciences*, **66B** (4), 478–89.

Downs, Anthony (1957), *An Economic Theory of Democracy*, New York: Harper & Row.

Duleep, Harriet Orcutt (1995), 'Mortality and income inequality among economically developed countries', *Social Security Bulletin*, **58** (2), 34–50.

d'Uva, T.B., O. O'Donnell and E. van Doorslaer (2008), 'Differential health reporting by education level and its impact on the measurement of health inequalities among older Europeans', *International Journal of Epidemiology*, **37** (6), 1375–83.

d'Uva, T.B., M. Lindeboom, O. O'Donnell and E. van Doorslaer (2009), 'Slipping anchor? Testing the vignettes approach to identification and correction of reporting heterogeneity', Health, Econometrics and Data Group (HEDG) working papers.

d'Uva, T.B., M. Lindeboom, O. O'Donnell and E. van Doorslaer (2011), 'Slipping anchor? Testing the vignettes approach to identification and correction of reporting heterogeneity', *Journal of Human Resources*, **46** (4), 875–906.

Edvinsson, S., E.H. Lundevaller and G. Malmberg (2013), 'Do unequal societies cause death among the elderly? A study of the health effects of inequality in Swedish municipalities in 2006', *Global Health Action*, 6.

Ehrlich, Isaac (1973), 'Participation in illegitimate activities: a theoretical and empirical investigation', *The Journal of Political Economy*, **81** (3), 521–65.

Fahey, T. and E. Smyth (2004), 'Do subjective indicators measure welfare? Evidence from 33 European societies', *European Societies*, **6** (1), 5–27.

Feng, Z., W.W. Wang, K. Jones and Y. Li (2012), 'An exploratory multilevel analysis of income, income inequality and self-rated health of the elderly in China', *Social Science & Medicine*, **75** (12), 2481–92.

Ferrer-i-Carbonell, A. and P. Frijters (2004), 'How important is methodology for the estimates of the determinants of happiness?' *Economic Journal*, **114** (497), 641–59.

Fiscella, K. and P. Franks (1997), 'Poverty or income inequality as predictor of mortality: Longitudinal Cohort Study', *British Medical Journal*, **314** (7096), 1724–7.

Fiscella, K. and P. Franks (2000), 'Individual income, income inequality, health, and mortality: what are the relationships?' *Health Services Research*, **35** (1, pt 2), 307–18.

Frank, R.H. (1985), *Choosing the Right Pond: Human Behavior and the Quest for Status*, New York and Oxford: Oxford University Press.

Frijters, P., J.P. Haisken-DeNew and M.A. Shields (2005), 'The causal effect of income on health: evidence from German reunification', *Journal of Health Economics*, **24** (5), 997–1017.

Fukuyama, Francis (1995), *Trust: The Social Virtues and the Creation of Prosperity*, New York: Free Press.

Gardner, Jonathan and Andrew J. Oswald (2007), 'Money and mental wellbeing: a longitudinal study of medium-sized lottery wins', *Journal of Health Economics*, **26** (1), 49–60.

Gerdtham, U. and Magnus Johannesson (2004), 'Absolute income, relative income, income inequality, and mortality', *Journal of Human Resources*, **39** (1), 228–47.

Goldthorpe, J.H. (2010), 'Analysing social inequality: a critique of two recent contributions from economics and epidemiology', *European Sociological Review*, **26** (6), 731–44.

Gravelle, H. (1998), 'How much of the relation between population mortality and unequal distribution of income is a statistical artefact?' *British Medical Journal*, **316** (7128), 382–5.

Gravelle, H. and M. Sutton (2009), 'Income, relative income, and self-reported health in Britain 1979–2000', *Health Economics*, **18** (2), 125.

Green, Geoff, J.M. Gilbertson and Michael F.J. Grimsley (2002), 'Fear of crime and health in residential tower blocks: a case study in Liverpool, UK', *European Journal of Public Health*, **12** (1), 10–15.

Grönqvist, H., P. Johansson and S. Niknami (2012), 'Income inequality and health: lessons from a refugee residential assignment program', *Journal of Health Economics*, **31** (4), 617–29.

Gustavsson, M. and H. Jordahl (2008), 'Inequality and trust in Sweden: some inequalities are more harmful than others', *Journal of Public Economics*, **92** (1–2), 348–65.

Haas, S.A. (2006), 'Health selection and the process of social stratification: the effect of childhood health on socioeconomic attainment', *Journal of Health and Social Behavior*, **47** (4), 339–54.

Haller, M. and M. Hadler (2006), 'How social relations and structures can produce happiness and unhappiness: an international comparative analysis', *Social Indicators Research*, **75** (2), 169–216.

Hammond, John L. (1973), 'Two sources of error in ecological correlations', *American Sociological Review*, **38** (6), 764–77.

Heckman, J.J. (2007), 'The economics, technology, and neuroscience of human capability formation', *Proceedings of the National Academy of Sciences of the United States of America*, **104** (33), 13250–55.

Henriksson, G., G.R. Weitoft and P. Allebeck (2010), 'Associations between income inequality at municipality level and health depend on context – a multilevel analysis on myocardial infarction in Sweden', *Social Science & Medicine*, **71** (6), 1141–9.

Hildebrand, V. and P. Van Kerm (2009), 'Income inequality and self-rated health status: evidence from the European Community Household Panel', *Demography*, **46** (4), 805–25.

Hirschman, A.O. (1973), 'The changing tolerance for income inequality in the course of economic development', *World Development*, **1** (12), 29–36.

Holstein, B.E., C. Currie, W. Boyce, M.T. Damsgaard, I. Gobina, G. Kökönyei, J. Hetland, M. de Looze, M. Richter, P. Due and HBSC Social Inequalities Focus Group (2009), 'Socio-economic inequality in multiple health complaints among adolescents: international comparative study in 37 countries', *International Journal of Public Health*, **54** (2), 260–70.

Ichida, Y., K. Kondo, H. Hirai, T. Hanibuchi, G. Yoshikawa and C. Murata (2009), 'Social capital, income inequality and self-rated health in Chita peninsula, Japan: a multilevel analysis of older people in 25 communities', *Social Science & Medicine*, **69** (4), 489–99.

Jen, M.H., K. Jones and R. Johnston (2009), 'Global variations in health: evaluating Wilkinson's income inequality hypothesis using the World Values Survey', *Social Science and Medicine*, **68** (4), 643–53.

Jenkins, Stephen P. (2015), 'World income inequality databases: an assessment of WIID and SWIID', *Journal of Economic Inequality*, **13** (4), 629–71.

Jenkins, Stephen P. and Philippe Van Kerm (2011), 'Trends in individual income growth: measurement methods and British evidence', Institute for Social and Economic Research, working paper series 2011–06.

Johnston, D.W., C. Propper and M.A. Shields (2009), 'Comparing subjective and objective measures of health: evidence from hypertension for the income/health gradient', *Journal of Health Economics*, **28** (3), 540–52.

Jones, A.M. and J. Wildman (2008), 'Health, income and relative deprivation: evidence from the BHPS', *Journal of Health Economics*, **27** (2), 308–24.

Jordahl, Henrik (2009), 'Economic inequality', in G.T. Svendsen and G.L.H. Svendsen (eds), *Handbook of Social Capital*, Cheltenham: Edward Elgar.

Jylhä, M. (2009), 'What is self-rated health and why does it predict mortality? Towards a unified conceptual model', *Social Science and Medicine*, **69** (3), 307–16.

Kahn, R.S., P.H. Wise, B.P. Kennedy and I. Kawachi (2000), 'State income inequality, household income, and maternal mental and physical health: cross-sectional national survey', *British Medical Journal*, **321** (7272), 1311–15.

Kaplan, G.A., E.R. Pamuk, J.W. Lynch, R.D. Cohen and J.L. Balfour (1996), 'Inequality in income and mortality in the United States: analysis of mortality and potential pathways', *British Medical Journal*, **312** (7037), 999–1003.

Karlsdotter, K., J.J. Martín Martín, and M.P. López del Amo González (2012), 'Multilevel analysis of income, income inequalities and health in Spain', *Social Science & Medicine*, **74** (7), 1099–106.

Karlsson, M., T. Nilsson, C.H. Lyttkens and G. Leeson (2010), 'Income inequality and health: importance of a cross-country perspective', *Social Science & Medicine*, **70** (6), 875–85.

Kawachi, I., S.V. Subramanian and D. Kim (2008), *Social Capital and Health*, Springer: New York.

Kennedy, B.P., I. Kawachi, R. Glass and D. Prothrow-Stith (1998), 'Income distribution, socioeconomic status, and self-rated health in the United States: multilevel analysis', *British Medical Journal*, **317** (7163), 917–21.

Knabe, Andreas, Steffen Rätzel, Ronnie Schöb and Joachim Weimann (2010), 'Dissatisfied with life but having a good day: time-use and well-being of the unemployed', *The Economic Journal*, **120** (547), 867–89.

Knight, J., L. Song and R. Gunatilaka (2009), 'Subjective well-being and its determinants in rural China', *China Economic Review*, **20** (4), 635–49.

Konow, J. (2000), 'Fair shares: accountability and cognitive dissonance in allocation decisions', *American Economic Review*, **90** (4), 1072–91.

Krugman, Paul (1996), 'The spiral of inequality', *Mother Jones*, **21**, 44–9.

Langbein, L. and A. Lichtman (1978), *Ecological Inference. Vol. 10 of Quantitative Applications in the Social Sciences*, Thousand Oaks, CA: Sage Publications.

Larren, C. and I. Kawachi (2005), 'Does economic inequality affect child malnutrition? The case of Ecuador', *Social Science & Medicine*, **60** (1), 165–78.

LeClere, Felicia B. and Mah-Jabeen Soobader (2000), 'The effect of income inequality on the health of selected US demographic groups', *American Journal of Public Health*, **90** (12), 1892–7.

Lee, L. (1982), 'Health and wage: a simultaneous equation model with multiple discrete indicators', *International Economic Review*, **23** (1), 199–222.

Leigh, A. and C. Jencks (2007), 'Inequality and mortality: long-run evidence from a panel of countries', *Journal of Health Economics*, **26** (1), 1–24.

Leigh, A., C. Jencks and T.M. Smeeding (2009), 'Health and economic inequality', in Salverda, W., B. Nolan and T. Smeeding (eds), *The Oxford Handbook of Economic Inequality*, Oxford: Oxford University Press.

Li, H. and Y. Zhu (2006), 'Income, income inequality, and health: evidence from China', *Journal of Comparative Economics*, **34** (4), 668–93.

Lillard, Dean R., R.V. Burkhauser, M.H. Hahn and R. Wilkins (2015), 'Does early-life income inequality predict self-reported health in later life? Evidence from the United States', *Social Science & Medicine*, **128**, 347–55.

Lin, Nan (1999), 'Social networks and status attainment', *Annual Review of Sociology*, **25** (1), 467–87.

Lindahl, M. (2005), 'Estimating the effect of income on health and mortality using lottery prizes as an exogenous source of variation in income', *Journal of Human Resources*, **40** (1), 144–68.

Link, B.G. and J. Phelan (1995), 'Social conditions as fundamental causes of disease', *Journal of Health and Social Behavior*, 80–94.

Ljungvall, Asa, Ulf G. Gerdtham and Ulf Lindblad (2015), 'Misreporting and misclassification: implications for socioeconomic disparities in body-mass index and obesity', *The European Journal of Health Economics*, **16** (1), 5–20.

Lochner, K., E. Pamuk, D. Makuc, B.P. Kennedy and I. Kawachi (2001), 'State-level income inequality and individual mortality risk: a prospective, multilevel study', *American Journal of Public Health*, **91** (3), 385–91.

Lorgelly, P.K. and J. Lindley (2008), 'What is the relationship between income inequality and health? Evidence from the BHPS', *Health Economics*, **17** (2), 249–65.

Luft, H.S. (1975), 'The impact of poor health on earnings', *Review of Economics & Statistics*, **57** (1), 43–58.

Lundberg, O., J. Fritzell, M. Yngwe and M.L. Kölegård (2010), 'The potential power of social policy programmes: income redistribution, economic resources and health', *International Journal of Social Welfare*, **19**, S2–S13.

Luttmer, E.F.P. (2005), 'Neighbors as negatives: relative earnings and well-being', *The Quarterly Journal of Economics*, **120** (3), 963–1002.

Lynch, J.W., G.D. Smith, G.A. Kaplan and J.S. House (2000), 'Income inequality and mortality: importance to health of individual income, psychosocial environment, or material conditions', *British Medical Journal*, **320** (7243), 1200–204.

Mackenbach, J.P. (2002), 'Income inequality and population health', *British Medical Journal*, **324** (7328), 1–2.

Marmot, M. (2010), *Fair Society, Healthy Lives: A Strategic Review of Health Inequalities in England Post-2010*, London: University College London, the Marmot Review.

Marmot, M.G., M.J. Shipley and G. Rose (1984), 'Inequalities in death–specific explanations of a general pattern?', *Lancet*, **1** (8384), 1003–1006.

Marmot, M.G., G.D. Smith, S. Stansfeld, C. Patel, F. North, J. Head, I. White, E. Brunner and A. Feeney (1991), 'Health

inequalities among British civil servants: the Whitehall II study',
Lancet, **337** (8754), 1387–93.

Martikainen, P., N. Mäki and J. Blomgren (2004), 'The effects of area
and individual social characteristics on suicide risk: a multilevel
study of relative contribution and effect modification', *European
Journal of Population/Revue Européenne de Démographie*, **20** (4),
323–50.

Mayer, Susanne and August Osterle (2015), 'Socioeconomic determinants of prescribed and non-prescribed medicine consumption in Austria', *The European Journal of Public Health*, **25** (4),
597–603.

McCloskey, D.N. and S.T. Ziliak (1996), 'The standard error of
regressions', *Journal of Economic Literature*, **34** (1), 97–114.

McLeod, C.B., J.N. Lavis, C.A. Mustard and G.L. Stoddart (2003),
'Income inequality, household income, and health status in
Canada: a prospective cohort study', *American Journal of Public
Health*, **93** (8), 1287–93.

Meara, Ellen (1999), *Inequality and Infant Health*, Harvard: Harvard
Medical School.

Mellor, Jennifer M. and Jeffrey Milyo (2002), 'Income inequality
and health status in the United States: evidence from the current
population survey', *Journal of Human Resources*, **37** (3), 510–39.

Mellor, Jennifer M. and Jeffrey Milyo (2003), 'Is exposure to income
inequality a public health concern? Lagged effects of income
inequality on individual and population health', *Health Services
Research*, **38** (1, 1), 137–51.

Merton, Robert King (1957), *Social Theory and Social Structure*,
Glencoe, IL: Free Press.

Merton, Robert King (1968), *Social Theory and Social Structure*,
New York: Free Press.

Miller, D.L. and C. Paxson (2006), 'Relative income, race, and mortality', *Journal of Health Economics*, **25** (5), 979–1003.

Milyo, Jeffrey D. and Jennifer M. Mellor (1999), 'Is inequality bad
for our health?' *Critical Review: A Journal of Politics and Society*,
13 (3–4), 359–72.

Nilsson, Anna (2004), 'Income inequality and crime: the case of
Sweden', IFAU working paper, 6.

Nilsson, Therese and Andreas Bergh (2014), 'Income inequality,
health and development – in search of a pattern', in Pedro Rosa
Dias and Owen O'Donnell (eds), *Health and Inequality (Research*

on Economic Inequality, Volume 21), Bingley, UK: Emerald Group Publishing Limited, 441–68.

O'Donnell, O., E. van Doorslaer and T. van Ourti (2014), 'Health and inequality' in A.B. Atkinson and F. Bourguignon (eds), *Handbook of Income Distribution*, SET vols 2A–2B, Elsevier, Amsterdam, ch. 17.

Oishi, S., S. Kesebir and E. Diener (2011), 'Income inequality and happiness', *Psychological Science*, **22** (9), 1095–100.

Oshio, T. and M. Kobayashi (2010), 'Income inequality, perceived happiness, and self-rated health: evidence from nationwide surveys in Japan', *Social Science and Medicine*, **70** (9), 1358–66.

Osler, M., E. Prescott, M. Grønbæk, U. Christensen, P. Due and G. Engholm (2002), 'Income inequality, individual income, and mortality in Danish adults: analysis of pooled data from two cohort studies', *British Medical Journal*, **324** (7328), 13–16.

Oster, Anna and Jonas Agell (2007), 'Crime and unemployment in turbulent times', *Journal of the European Economic Association*, **5** (4), 752–75.

Pampel, F.C. Jr and V.K. Pillai (1986), 'Patterns and determinants of infant mortality in developed nations, 1950–1975', *Demography*, **23** (4), 525–42.

Paulus, Alari, Holly Sutherland and Panos Tsakloglou (2010), 'The distributional impact of in-kind public benefits in European countries', *Journal of Policy Analysis and Management*, **29** (2), 243–66.

Pendakur, Krishna (2002), 'Taking prices seriously in the measurement of inequality', *Journal of Public Economics*, **86** (47), 69.

Pickett, Kate E. and Richard G. Wilkinson (2015), 'Income inequality and health: a causal review', *Social Science & Medicine*, **128**, 316–26.

Pickett, Kate E., Shona Kelly, Eric Brunner, Tim Lobstein and Richard G. Wilkinson (2005), 'Wider income gaps, wider waistbands? An ecological study of obesity and income inequality', *Journal of Epidemiology and Community Health*, **59** (8), 670–4.

Redelmeier, D.A. and S.M. Singh (2001), 'Survival in Academy Award-winning actors and actresses', *Annals of Internal Medicine*, **134** (10), 955–62.

Rice, N., S. Robone and P. Smith (2010), 'Analysis of the validity of the vignette approach to correct for heterogeneity in reporting health system responsiveness', *European Journal of Health Economics*, **12** (2), 141–62.

Robinson, W.S. (1950), 'Ecological correlations and the behavior of individuals', *American Sociological Review*, **15** (3), 351–7.

Rodgers, G.B. (1979), 'Income and inequality as determinants of mortality: an international cross-section analysis', *Population Studies*, **33** (2), 343–51.

Roemer, J.E. (1996), *Theories of Distributive Justice*, Cambridge, MA: Harvard University Press.

Roine, J. and D. Waldenström (2015), 'Long-run trends in the distribution of income and wealth', in A. Atkinson and F. Bourguignon (eds), *Handbook in Income Distribution*, vol. 2A, Amsterdam: North-Holland.

Rostila, M., M.L. Kölegård and J. Fritzell (2012), 'Income inequality and self-rated health in Stockholm, Sweden: a test of the "income inequality hypothesis" on two levels of aggregation', *Social Science & Medicine*, **74** (7), 1091–8.

Rözer, Jesper and Gerbert Kraaykamp (2013), 'Income inequality and subjective well-being: a cross-national study on the conditional effects of individual and national characteristics', *Social Indicators Research*, **113** (3), 1009–23.

Rufrancos, H.G., M. Power, K.E. Pickett and R. Wilkinson (2013), 'Income inequality and crime: a review and explanation of the time-series evidence', *Social Crimonol*, **1**, 103.

Ruhm, C.J. (2000), 'Are recessions good for your health?' *The Quarterly Journal of Economics*, **115** (2), 617–50.

Ruhm, C.J. (2005), 'Healthy living in hard times', *Journal of Health Economics*, **24** (2), 341–63.

Runciman, W.E. (1966), *Relative Deprivation and Social Justice: A Study of Attitudes to Social Inequality in Twentieth-Century England*, Berkeley: University of California Press.

Sadana, R., C.D. Mathers, A.D. Lopez, C.J.L. Murray and K. Iburg (2000), 'Comparative analysis of more than 50 household surveys on health status', GPE discussion paper, World Health Organization.

Salomon, J.A., A. Tandon and C.J. Murray (2004), 'Comparability of self-rated health: cross-sectional multi-country survey using anchoring vignettes', *British Medical Journal*, **328** (7434), 258.

Sapolsky, R.M., S.C. Alberts and J. Altmann (1997), 'Hypercortisolism associated with social subordinance or social isolation among wild baboons', *Archives of General Psychiatry*, **54** (12), 1137–43.

Schaller, J. and A.H. Stevens (2015), 'Short-run effects of job loss on health conditions, health insurance, and health care utilization', *Journal of Health Economics*, **43**, 190–203.

Schwarze, J. and M. Härpfer (2007), 'Are people inequality averse, and do they prefer redistribution by the state? Evidence from German longitudinal data on life satisfaction', *Journal of Socio-Economics*, **36** (2), 233–49.

Sen, A. (1992), *Inequality Reexamined*, Oxford: Oxford University Press.

Senik, C. (2004), 'When information dominates comparison: learning from Russian subjective panel data', *Journal of Public Economics*, **88** (9–10), 2099–123.

Senik, C. (2009), 'Direct evidence on income comparisons and their welfare effects', *Journal of Economic Behavior and Organization*, **72** (1), 408–24.

Shi, L. and B. Starfield (2000), 'Primary care, income inequality, and self-rated health in the United States: a mixed-level analysis', *International Journal of Health Services*, **30** (3), 541–55.

Shibuya, K., H. Hashimoto and E. Yano (2002), 'Individual income, income distribution, and self-rated health in Japan: cross-sectional analysis of nationally representative sample', *British Medical Journal*, **324** (7328), 16–19.

Siegman, A.W. (1994), 'Cardiovascular consequences of expressing and repressing anger', in A.W. Siegman and T.W. Smith (eds), *Anger, Hostility, and the Heart*, New Jersey: Lawrence Erlbaum, 173–97.

Slesnick, Daniel T. (2001), *Consumption and Social Welfare*, Cambridge: Cambridge University Press.

Solt, Frederick (2009), 'Standardizing the World Income Inequality Database', *Social Science Quarterly*, **90** (2), 231–42.

Solt, Frederick (2016), 'On the assessment and use of cross-national income inequality datasets', *Journal of Economic Inequality* (forthcoming).

Soobader, M.J. and F.B. LeClere (1999), 'Aggregation and the measurement of income inequality: effects on morbidity', *Social Science and Medicine*, **48** (6), 733–44.

Statistics Sweden (2003), Statisikdatabasen, http://www.scb.se/.

Statistics Sweden (2010), Statisikdatabasen, http://www.scb.se/.

Statistics Sweden (2011), Statisikdatabasen, http://www.scb.se/.

Statistiska Centralbyrån (2010), *Tabeller över Sveriges befolkning 2009*, Örebro: Statistiska Centralbyrån.

Sturm, R. and C.R. Gresenz (2002), 'Relations of income inequality and family income to chronic medical conditions and mental health disorders: national survey', *British Medical Journal*, **324** (7328), 20–23.

Subramanian, S.V. and Ichiro Kawachi (2004), 'Income inequality and health: what have we learned so far?' *Epidemiologic Reviews*, **26** (1), 78–91.

Subramanian, S.V. and I. Kawachi (2006), 'Whose health is affected by income inequality? A multilevel interaction analysis of contemporaneous and lagged effects of state income inequality on individual self-rated health in the United States', *Health and Place*, **12** (2), 141–56.

Subramanian, S.V., I. Delgado, L. Jadue, J. Vega and I. Kawachi (2003), 'Income inequality and health: multilevel analysis of Chilean communities', *Journal of Epidemiology and Community Health*, **57** (11), 844–8.

Subramanian, S.V., I Kawachi and B.P. Kennedy (2001), 'Does the state you live in make a difference? Multilevel analysis of self-rated health in the US', *Social Science & Medicine*, **53** (1), 9–19.

Subramanian, S.V., I. Kawachi and G.D. Smith (2007), 'Income inequality and the double burden of under- and overnutrition in India', *Journal of Epidemiology and Community Health*, **61** (9), 802–9.

Swedish National Board of Health and Welfare (2011), Statistikdatabas för cancer, http://www.socialstyrelsen.se/statis tik/statistikdatabas/cancer.

Sylvestre, Marie-Pierre, Ella Huszti and James A. Hanley (2006), 'Do Oscar winners live longer than less successful peers? A reanalysis of the evidence', *Annals of Internal Medicine*, **145** (5), 361–3.

Sylvestre, M-P., E. Huszti and J.A. Hanley (2006), 'Do Oscar winners live longer than less successful peers? A reanalysis of the evidence', *Annals of Internal Medicine*, **145** (5), 361–3.

Tåhlin, M. (2007), 'Class clues', *European Sociological Review*, **23** (5), 557–72.

Tandon, A., C.J.L. Murray, J.A. Salomon and G. King (2003), 'Statistical models for enhancing cross-population comparability', in C.J.L. Murray and D.B. Evans (eds), *Health Systems*

Performance Assessment: Debates, Methods and Empiricisms, Geneva, Switzerland: World Health Organization, 727–46.

Tomes, N. (1986), 'Income distribution, happiness and satisfaction: a direct test of the interdependent preferences model', *Journal of Economic Psychology*, **7** (4), 425–46.

Vågerö, D. (2011), 'En folkhälsopolitisk kardinalfråga: ökade sociala skillnader in dödlighet under fyra decennier', *Socialmedicinsk Tidskrift*, 292–8.

Verme, P. (2011), 'Life satisfaction and income inequality', *Review of Income and Wealth*, **57** (1), 111–27.

Wagstaff, A. and E. van Doorslaer (2000), 'Income inequality and health: what does the literature tell us?' *Annual Review of Public Health*, **21**, 543–67.

Waldenström, Daniel (2009), *Lifting All Boats? The Evolution of Income and Wealth Inequality Over the Path of Development*, Doktorsavhandling in Ekonomisk Historia, Lund: Media-Tryck, Lunds Universitet.

Wang, P., J. Pan and Z. Luo (2015), 'The impact of income inequality on individual happiness: evidence from China', *Social Indicators Research*, **121** (2), 413–35.

Ware, J.E., M. Kosinski, J.E. Dewey and B. Gandek (2000), *SF-36 Health Survey: Manual and Interpretation Guide*, Quality Metric Inc.

Weich, S., G. Lewis and S.P. Jenkins (2001), 'Income inequality and the prevalence of common mental disorders in Britain: the *British Journal of Psychiatry*', *The Journal of Mental Science*, **178**, 222–7.

Weich, S., G. Lewis and S.P. Jenkins (2002), 'Income inequality and self-rated health in Britain', *Journal of Epidemiology & Community Health*, **56** (6), 436–41.

Wilkinson, R.G. (1996), *Unhealthy Societies: The Afflictions of Inequality*, London: Routledge.

Wilkinson, R.G. (1997), 'Socioeconomic determinants of health: health inequalities: relative or absolute material standards?' *British Medical Journal*, **314** (7080), 591.

Wilkinson, R.G. and K. Pickett (1996), *Unhealthy Societies: The Afflictions of Inequality*, London: Routledge.

Wilkinson, R.G. and K. Pickett (2009), *The Spirit Level: Why More Equal Societies Almost Always Do Better*, London: Allen Lane.

Wilkinson, R.G. and K. Pickett (2010), *Jämlikhetsanden: därför är ner jämlika samhällen nästan alltid bättre samhällen* (L. Ohlsson trans.), Stockholm: Karneval.

Wilkinson, Richard G. (1986), *Class and Health: Research and Longitudinal Data*, Tavistock: Economic and Social Research Council.

Wilkinson, Richard G. and Kate E. Pickett (2006), 'Income inequality and population health: a review and explanation of the evidence', *Social Science & Medicine*, **62** (7), 1768–84.

Williams, J.E., C.C. Paton, I.C. Siegler, M.L. Eigenbrodt, F.J. Nieto and H.A. Tyroler (2000), 'Anger proneness predicts coronary heart disease risk: prospective analysis from the Atherosclerosis Risk in Communities (ARIC) study', *Circulation*, **101** (17), 2034–9.

Wong, I.O.L., B.J. Cowling, S. Lo and G.M. Leung (2009), 'A multilevel analysis of the effects of neighbourhood income inequality on individual self-rated health in Hong Kong', *Social Science & Medicine*, **68** (1), 124–32.

Yngwe, M.A., J. Fritzell, O. Lundberg, F. Diderichsen and B. Burström (2003), 'Exploring relative deprivation: is social comparison a mechanism in the relation between income and health?', *Social Science & Medicine*, **57** (8), 1463–73.

Yngwe, M.A., J. Fritzell, B. Burström and O. Lundberg (2005), 'Comparison or consumption? Distinguishing between different effects of income on health in Nordic welfare states', *Social Science & Medicine*, **61** (3), 627–35.

Zagorski, Krzysztof, M.D.R. Evans, J. Kelley and K. Piotrowska (2014), 'Does national income inequality affect individuals' quality of life in Europe? Inequality, happiness, finances, and health', *Social Indicators Research*, **117** (3), 1089–110.

Zheng, H. (2009), 'Rising US income inequality, gender and individual self-rated health, 1972–2004', *Social Science & Medicine*, **69** (9), 1333–42.

Zheng, H. (2012), 'Do people die from income inequality of a decade ago?' *Social Science & Medicine*, **75** (1), 36–45.

Zheng, H. and L.K. George (2012), 'Rising US income inequality and the changing gradient of socioeconomic status on physical functioning and activity limitations, 1984–2007', *Social Science & Medicine*, **75** (12), 2170–82.

Index

160 *Sick of inequality?*

Printed and bound by CPI Group (UK) Ltd, Croydon, CR0 4YY

23/04/2025

14660980-0002